Old Palace of John Whitgift School
Independent Girls' School

WITHDRAWN FROM STOCK

Tel: 0208 688 2027

Date of issue	Student name	form
Sep '19	Isra Chaudhry	12

PASSPORT STUDY NOTES

Copyright © 2016 Chris Webster

ISBN: 1534821988
ISBN-13: 978-1534821989

DISCLAIMER

The publisher has made every effort to ensure that these notes conform to the current OIB and OCR syllabuses, and that the text of the poems is accurate. However, teachers are advised to check the latest version of their syllabus, and to teach from the prescribed/recommended editions.

The cover design is based on an unfinished portrait of Christina Rossetti by John Brett.

DEDICATION

For my OIB class of 2016-17. Enjoy – or try to!

CONTENTS

Introduction

These study notes were written for the OIB (Option Internationale du Baccalauréat) and OCR A-level examinations. They include a biography, questions on the poems, commentaries and sample examination questions. The full text of all the set poems for both examinations is included. The contents page shows which poems are set for each examination, but it is recommended that students read them all, though focusing in detail on the list set for the examination they will be taking. This is important because the OIB syllabus contains only two devotional poems, and the OCR syllabus lacks some of the most powerful love poems.

The study notes are suitable for both individual and class use. When used in class, one approach would be read the poem with the students then ask them to work through the questions in pairs or small groups. When they have finished, discuss their responses. Only then should the commentaries be read and discussed. On occasions students could be asked to follow up the lesson with different kinds of writing. Sometimes this will be a response to some or all of the questions. Sometimes they could be asked to write their own commentary on a poem (without reading the commentary in the book).

The essay and examination questions at the end of the book can be used in a number of ways: students could be asked to present an essay topic to the class, for example, in a PowerPoint presentation. They can also be used for homework essays and practice under examination conditions.

Biography

The purpose of this brief biography is to relate the poems in this volume to Rossetti's life. This is never an easy thing to do as it is not always clear whether the voice in a poem is Rossetti's, or whether it is written from the point of view of a persona, as is so often the case, particularly with love poetry. Another problem is that the selection of poems in this book is a very small (though representative) proportion of her huge output. Nevertheless, it is useful to construct a hypothetical link as it helps the student to consider the poems as a whole. The important point is, unless there is a clear link with Rossetti's life, which is sometime given us by the writings of her brother, William Rossetti, any links that are made in essays should be written in tentative language, i.e., "it is possible that…", "this poem may relate to the period in Rossetti's life when…" etc.

Christina Rossetti was born in 1830 in London to Gabriele Rossetti, a painter and a political exile from Italy. She had two brothers, Dante Gabriel, and William Michael, and a sister, Maria. She was educated at home and exposed to a wide range of liberal, enlightened ideas. As a result, she was opposed to war, slavery, cruelty to animals, the exploitation of girls in under-age prostitution, the subservient position of women in marriage, and all forms of military aggression. Her childhood seems to have been a happy one, but in the 1840s, her family faced financial difficulties due to the deterioration of her father's health. In 1843, He gave up his teaching post at King's College and Rossetti's mother began teaching to keep the family. When she was 14, Rossetti suffered a nervous breakdown and left school. Thereafter she led a very retiring life, interrupted by a recurring illness which was sometimes diagnosed as angina and sometimes tuberculosis. During this period she, her mother, and her sister became deeply interested in the Anglo-Catholic movement in the Church of England. Rossetti became a devout Christian. We can see evidence of this in her poems, where she shows a very detailed knowledge of the Bible. See, for example, her description of Paradise in the poem of that name, which is built up from several Biblical sources. Throughout her life Rossetti wrote many devotional poems in which she expresses her beliefs, hopes and doubts. For example *In the Bleak Midwinter* expresses her belief in the Nativity stories, the two poems about Paradise express a beatific vision of Heaven, and *Shut Out* expresses doubts that she is worthy of salvation.

She wrote poetry from an early age, and in 1847 her grandfather paid for her first book of poems, *Verses*, to be published.

In 1848, her brother, Dante Gabriel became (with William Holman Hunt and John Everett Millais) one of the founding members of The Pre-Raphaelite Brotherhood (PRB) . They were later joined by William Michael Rossetti, James Collinson, Frederic George Stephens and Thomas Woolner. Rossetti was not allowed to be a member because she was a woman. Nevertheless, she contributed some poetry to their magazine, *The Germ*. Rossetti fell in love with and got engaged to Collinson in the same year.

In 1849 Rossetti was seriously ill again, and in this year she wrote *Remember*. Clearly, she feared that she might die, and did not wish her loved ones to grieve for her.

In 1850 her engagement to Collinson was broken off because of a conflict over religious belief. He had originally been a Catholic, but converted to Anglicanism in order to marry Rossetti, but when he reverted to Catholicism because of his conscience, she broke off the engagement. According to William Michael, this was "a blow from which she did not fully recover for years". This can be seen in many later poems which reflect, directly or indirectly on this relationship. The doctrinal differences between a High Church Anglican and a Catholic are very small, and it is hard to believe that someone would break off an engagement because of them.

1850 must have been an exciting year for Rossetti because the painter John Brett proposed to her. Her rejection of him is immortalised in the poem *No, Thank you, John* (written in 1860). That the John of the poem is John Brett is confirmed in the writings of William Michael.

In 1853, Rossetti wrote a poem about the breakup of the PRB – prematurely, as it happened, for the artists in the movement were to go on to great things. Another poem about the PRB is *In an Artist's Studio*. This describes her brother's obsession with his model Elizabeth Siddal.

In 1854, Rossetti wrote several poems that seem to suggest she was regretting her lost chances of love, among them *From the Antique* and *Echo*. She would continue to write poems on this theme for the rest of her life.

In 1856 Rossetti wrote *Love from the North* which is one of her many poems about the rejection of lovers. The woman in the poem is actually in the middle of the wedding ceremony, so it could be based on a memory of her broken engagement to Collinson. The woman's attraction to the man from the north can be seen as an example of 'bad boy' syndrome. Is this what Rossetti yearned for subconsciously? A masterful, exciting lover, who take her to faraway and dangerous places.

1857 was the year of the Indian Mutiny about which Rossetti wrote a moving poem about a husband and wife who commit suicide (*In the Round Tower at Jhansi*). In this year she met Charles Bagot Cayley (1823-1883) who was a poet and translator. He quickly fell in love with her. It was in this year she also wrote *A Birthday*, which celebrates the coming of love, so the poem could refer to him, but she rejected his suit because he was an agnostic.

In 1859 Rossetti started volunteer work in homes for "fallen women" (prostitutes), and some say that this may have been reflected in the sin and redemption, and sexual themes in Goblin Market.

In 1862 *Gobin Market and Other Poems* was published to great acclaim. Indeed, after Elizabeth Barrett Browning's death two months later, she was hailed as her natural successor as "female laureate", and was actually considered for that honour when the then Poet Laureate, Tennyson, died. In the event the honour was offered to a male poet, Alfred Austin, who, though he had a magnificent moustache, is little-remembered today.

In 1866 she published *The Prince's Progress and Other Poems*. The title poem is a long narrative poem which attempts to be another *Goblin Market*, but is less successful. One of the best poems in this collection is *Jessie Cameron* in which a woman called Jessie rejects the love of a young neighbour in words that recall *No, Thank You, John*. The collection also includes *Somewhere or Other*. In this poem Rossetti wonders where that special person, that "soulmate" is, whom she had not met. Perhaps she set the bar too high, or perhaps she was not prepared to compromise. Or perhaps it was because of what one critic has described as "the oppressive load of religious ideas" (Humphries, 2008) that dominated her life and work.

In 1872 she was diagnosed with Grave's Disease, an auto-immune disease that affects the thyroid. In the same year she published *Sing-Song*, a book of illustrated nursery rhymes. She also wrote more and more religious poetry, including the very fine *In the Bleak Midwinter*.

Rossetti campaigned vigorously for a range of social causes, and held strong opinions on the position of women in society, yet when a fellow poet, Augusta Webster, asked her to support the Suffrage Bill of 1878, Rossetti refused because of her Christian values, and the clear message in the Bible that women are subservient to and should obey men.

In 1890 she wrote *A Daughter of Eve* in which she laments the loneliness she faces and upbraids herself for not seizing the opportunities of her "summer", her youth. Did she perhaps remember one of her suitors with a particular fondness? *Soeur Louise de la Misericorde* is an even more powerful poem on the same theme.

In 1893 she was diagnosed with Breast Cancer, and though the tumour was removed, she suffered a relapse and died in 1894.

Love From The North

I had a love in soft south land,
Beloved through April far in May;
He waited on my lightest breath,
And never dared to say me nay.

He saddened if my cheer was sad,
But gay he grew if I was gay;
We never differed on a hair,
My yes his yes, my nay his nay.

The wedding hour was come, the aisles
Were flushed with sun and flowers that day;
I pacing balanced in my thoughts:
"It's quite too late to think of nay."–

My bridegroom answered in his turn,
Myself had almost answered "yea:"
When through the flashing nave I heard
A struggle and resounding "nay."

Bridemaids and bridegroom shrank in fear,
But I stood high who stood at bay:
"And if I answer yea, fair Sir,
What man art thou to bar with nay?"

He was a strong man from the north,
Light-locked, with eyes of dangerous grey:
"Put yea by for another time
In which I will not say thee nay."

He took me in his strong white arms,
He bore me on his horse away

O'er crag, morass, and hairbreadth pass,
But never asked me yea or nay.

He made me fast with book and bell,
With links of love he makes me stay;
Till now I've neither heart nor power
Nor will nor wish to say him nay.

QUESTIONS

1. What story does the poem tell?

2. Who seems to be the dominant partner in each of the
   woman's relationships? What is the evidence for this?

3. What does the phrase "I pacing balanced in my
   thoughts" tell us about the woman's feelings about the
   marriage?

4. What are the qualities of the man from the north that
   the woman finds attractive?

5. Why did she stay with him?

6. Describe the verse form. Count the stressed syllables in
   each line of the first stanza. What is the rhyme scheme
   of the first stanza? How is rhyme used throughout the
   poem as a whole? What words does it emphasise? Why
   is this important?

7. What opposites can you find in the poem?

8. How is the word "nay" used differently throughout the
   poem?

9. Explain the following metaphorical expressions:

- the flashing nave
- light-locked
- hairbreadth pass
- book and bell
- links of love

10. Is it possible to relate this poem to Rossetti's life?

11. Is this a poem about "bad boy syndrome"? Read this explanation of the syndrome and then discuss:

Women like bad boys because they're downright fascinating. While 'bad guys' are selfish, rule-breaking, imprudent, and rebellious, they are also brave, temerarious, independent, and self-reliant— and they live frantic, galvanizing lives. Bad boys are fun, and like Cyndi Lauper said, girls just want to have fun. 'Nice guys' just can't offer women any of the thrills their dominant, leather jacket-wearing counterparts can. (Evolution & Human Behavior, 2015, by Corinna E. Löckenhoff)

To what extent is this psychological syndrome (the bad boy syndrome) operating in this poem?

12. How might a feminist respond to this poem? Why might she enjoy *Outlandish Knight* more? (see below)

13. Compare and contrast this poem to the English folk ballad *Outlandish Knight*.

9

Outlandish Knight

An outlandish knight from the north lands came,
And he came a wooing me.
He promised heed take me unto the northern lands
And there he'd marry me.

"Come fetch me some of your father's gold,
And some of your mother's fee,
And two of the best horses in the stable
Where there stand thirty and three."

He mounted on the milk white steed
And she on the dappled gray,
And they rode till they came to the salt water side
An hour before the day.

"Light off, light off your steed," he said,
"And deliver it unto me.
For six pretty maidens I have drowned here,
And you the seventh shall be.

"Pull off, pull off thy silken gown,
And deliver it unto me;
Methinks it looks too rich and too gay
To rot in the salt sea,"

"Pull off, pull off thy silken stays,
And deliver it unto me;
Methinks they are too fine and gay
To rot in the salt sea,"

"Take off, take off your Holland smock
And deliver it unto me.

For it is too fine and too rich a gear
To rot with you under the sea."

"If I must take off my Holland smock
Then turn your face from me.
For it is not fitting that such a ruffian
A naked lady should see."

So he's turned his face away from her
To view the leaves so green,
And she's catched him by the middle so small
And she's tumbled him into the stream.

Well he swam high and he swam low,
Till he came unto the side,
"Fetch hold of my hand you pretty fair maid
And I will make you my bride."

"Lie there, lie there you false hearted man!
Lie there instead of me!
For if six pretty maidens you have drowned there,
The seventh one hath drowned thee!"

NOTE

You might also enjoy listening to this popular song on a
similar theme: *It Should Have Been Me* (1963) by William
"Mickey" Stevenson and Norman Whitfield for Kim
Weston. It has been performed by Yvonne Fair, Gladys
Knight & the Pips and Adeva among others.

COMMENTARY

Love From The North is written in stanzas consisting of
four tetrameters with a rhyme scheme of a b c b, the b
rhyme continuing throughout the poem along with the

word "nay" in the last line of each stanza, which is a kind of refrain, and has the effect of giving the poem a haunting unity. The poem shows the influence of ballads, both in form and content, and may have been inspired by the ballad *Outlandish Knight*, which has a similar subject.

The poem describes a love affair in the "soft south" – the north has always been seen as hard from the time of the raids by Picts and Scots, to the "dark, satanic mills" of the industrial revolution. It was a short romance (April to May) and her lover was totally compliant to her moods and wishes. The word "nay" is first introduced at the end of the first stanza to show how compliant he is. By the third stanza, she is about to be married and experiencing doubts. The word "nay" now becomes the impossible response to the wedding vow. The actual words of the ceremony in Victorian England were:

Wilt thou have this man to thy wedded husband, to live together after God's ordinance in the holy estate of Matrimony? Wilt thou obey him, and serve him, love, honour, and keep him, in sickness and in health; and, forsaking all other, keep thee only unto him, so long as ye both shall live?"

To which the answer is: "I will" (not "yea").

Discuss the use of the word "obey" in this vow.

Stanza four describes that the bridegroom had made his answer and she was about to make hers, when a 'resounding' voice shouts "nay". She proudly challenges him, but the first lines of stanza six show that she finds him fascinating. The word "dangerous" suggests that this might be the "bad boy syndrome" (see above) at work. The next stanza shows that he is exciting (he takes he to wild and dangerous places, and dominant (unlike her first lover). The

12

last stanza shows how complete her submission is, though note the title of the poem, where the word "love" is used.

Is this the kind of relationship that Rossetti yearned for, and why she rejected three suitors?

It is interesting to compare *Outlandish Knight*. As in Rossetti's poem, the knight is a mysterious stranger from the wild north. The verse form is similar, though used with more flexibility in the ballad. Like the stranger in Rossetti's poem, he wants to dominate her. He orders her to strip, after which we guess he will have his way, and then, like six others, he will drown her. But, unlike the woman in Rossetti's poem, she gets the better of him and drowns him instead.

The song, *It Should Have Been Me*, is merely an amusing sidelight on the topic. Students might also enjoy Chapter XXVI of *Jane Eyre* by Charlotte Bronte, when Mr Biggs, a London solicitor, interrupts Jayne Eyre's marriage to declare an "impediment" (a legal objection).

Goblin Market

NOTE: This is the full version of the poem. Another version, shortened for study purposes, follows. Read this version first, then go to the study version. You may wish to come back to this version for further in-depth study. WARNING: the questions and commentary contain adult themes.

Morning and evening
Maids heard the goblins cry:
"Come buy our orchard fruits,
Come buy, come buy:
Apples and quinces,
Lemons and oranges,
Plump unpecked cherries,
Melons and raspberries,
Bloom-down-cheeked peaches,
Swart-headed mulberries,
Wild free-born cranberries,
Crab-apples, dewberries,
Pine-apples, blackberries,
Apricots, strawberries;–
All ripe together
In summer weather,–
Morns that pass by,
Fair eves that fly;
Come buy, come buy:
Our grapes fresh from the vine,
Pomegranates full and fine,
Dates and sharp bullaces,
Rare pears and greengages,
Damsons and bilberries,
Taste them and try:

Currants and gooseberries,
Bright-fire-like barberries,
Figs to fill your mouth,
Citrons from the South,
Sweet to tongue and sound to eye;
Come buy, come buy."

Evening by evening
Among the brookside rushes,
Laura bowed her head to hear,
Lizzie veiled her blushes:
Crouching close together
In the cooling weather,
With clasping arms and cautioning lips,
With tingling cheeks and finger tips.
"Lie close," Laura said,
Pricking up her golden head:
"We must not look at goblin men,
We must not buy their fruits:
Who knows upon what soil they fed
Their hungry thirsty roots?"
"Come buy," call the goblins
Hobbling down the glen.

"Oh," cried Lizzie, "Laura, Laura,
You should not peep at goblin men."
Lizzie covered up her eyes,
Covered close lest they should look;
Laura reared her glossy head,
And whispered like the restless brook:
"Look, Lizzie, look, Lizzie,
Down the glen tramp little men.
One hauls a basket,
One bears a plate,
One lugs a golden dish
Of many pounds weight.

How fair the vine must grow
Whose grapes are so luscious;
How warm the wind must blow
Through those fruit bushes."
"No," said Lizzie, "No, no, no;
Their offers should not charm us,
Their evil gifts would harm us."
She thrust a dimpled finger
In each ear, shut eyes and ran:
Curious Laura chose to linger
Wondering at each merchant man.
One had a cat's face,
One whisked a tail,
One tramped at a rat's pace,
One crawled like a snail,
One like a wombat prowled obtuse and furry,
One like a ratel tumbled hurry skurry.
She heard a voice like voice of doves
Cooing all together:
They sounded kind and full of loves
In the pleasant weather.

Laura stretched her gleaming neck
Like a rush-imbedded swan,
Like a lily from the beck,
Like a moonlit poplar branch,
Like a vessel at the launch
When its last restraint is gone.

Backwards up the mossy glen
Turned and trooped the goblin men,
With their shrill repeated cry,
"Come buy, come buy."
When they reached where Laura was
They stood stock still upon the moss,
Leering at each other,

Brother with queer brother;
Signalling each other,
Brother with sly brother.
One set his basket down,
One reared his plate;
One began to weave a crown
Of tendrils, leaves, and rough nuts brown
(Men sell not such in any town);
One heaved the golden weight
Of dish and fruit to offer her:
"Come buy, come buy," was still their cry.
Laura stared but did not stir,
Longed but had no money:
The whisk-tailed merchant bade her taste
In tones as smooth as honey,
The cat-faced purred,
The rat-faced spoke a word
Of welcome, and the snail-paced even was heard;
One parrot-voiced and jolly
Cried "Pretty Goblin" still for "Pretty Polly;"–
One whistled like a bird.

But sweet-tooth Laura spoke in haste:
"Good folk, I have no coin;
To take were to purloin:
I have no copper in my purse,
I have no silver either,
And all my gold is on the furze
That shakes in windy weather
Above the rusty heather."
"You have much gold upon your head,"
They answered all together:
"Buy from us with a golden curl."
She clipped a precious golden lock,
She dropped a tear more rare than pearl,
Then sucked their fruit globes fair or red:

Sweeter than honey from the rock,
Stronger than man-rejoicing wine,
Clearer than water flowed that juice;
She never tasted such before,
How should it cloy with length of use?
She sucked and sucked and sucked the more
Fruits which that unknown orchard bore;
She sucked until her lips were sore;
Then flung the emptied rinds away
But gathered up one kernel stone,
And knew not was it night or day
As she turned home alone.

Lizzie met her at the gate
Full of wise upbraidings:
"Dear, you should not stay so late,
Twilight is not good for maidens;
Should not loiter in the glen
In the haunts of goblin men.
Do you not remember Jeanie,
How she met them in the moonlight,
Took their gifts both choice and many,
Ate their fruits and wore their flowers
Plucked from bowers
Where summer ripens at all hours?
But ever in the noonlight
She pined and pined away;
Sought them by night and day,
Found them no more, but dwindled and grew grey;
Then fell with the first snow,
While to this day no grass will grow
Where she lies low:
I planted daisies there a year ago
That never blow.
You should not loiter so."
"Nay, hush," said Laura:

"Nay, hush, my sister:
I ate and ate my fill,
Yet my mouth waters still;
To-morrow night I will
Buy more;" and kissed her:
"Have done with sorrow;
I'll bring you plums to-morrow
Fresh on their mother twigs,
Cherries worth getting;
You cannot think what figs
My teeth have met in,
What melons icy-cold
Piled on a dish of gold
Too huge for me to hold,
What peaches with a velvet nap,
Pellucid grapes without one seed:
Odorous indeed must be the mead
Whereon they grow, and pure the wave they drink
With lilies at the brink,
And sugar-sweet their sap."

Golden head by golden head,
Like two pigeons in one nest
Folded in each other's wings,
They lay down in their curtained bed:
Like two blossoms on one stem,
Like two flakes of new-fallen snow,
Like two wands of ivory
Tipped with gold for awful kings.
Moon and stars gazed in at them,
Wind sang to them lullaby,
Lumbering owls forbore to fly,
Not a bat flapped to and fro
Round their rest:
Cheek to cheek and breast to breast
Locked together in one nest.

Early in the morning
When the first cock crowed his warning,
Neat like bees, as sweet and busy,
Laura rose with Lizzie:
Fetched in honey, milked the cows,
Aired and set to rights the house,
Kneaded cakes of whitest wheat,
Cakes for dainty mouths to eat,
Next churned butter, whipped up cream,
Fed their poultry, sat and sewed;
Talked as modest maidens should:
Lizzie with an open heart,
Laura in an absent dream,
One content, one sick in part;
One warbling for the mere bright day's delight,
One longing for the night.

At length slow evening came:
They went with pitchers to the reedy brook;
Lizzie most placid in her look,
Laura most like a leaping flame.
They drew the gurgling water from its deep;
Lizzie plucked purple and rich golden flags,
Then turning homeward said: "The sunset flushes
Those furthest loftiest crags;
Come, Laura, not another maiden lags.
No wilful squirrel wags,
The beasts and birds are fast asleep."
But Laura loitered still among the rushes
And said the bank was steep.

And said the hour was early still
The dew not fallen, the wind not chill;
Listening ever, but not catching
The customary cry,
"Come buy, come buy,"

With its iterated jingle
Of sugar-baited words:
Not for all her watching
Once discerning even one goblin
Racing, whisking, tumbling, hobbling;
Let alone the herds
That used to tramp along the glen,
In groups or single,
Of brisk fruit-merchant men.

Till Lizzie urged, "O Laura, come;
I hear the fruit-call but I dare not look:
You should not loiter longer at this brook:
Come with me home.
The stars rise, the moon bends her arc,
Each glowworm winks her spark,
Let us get home before the night grows dark:
For clouds may gather
Though this is summer weather,
Put out the lights and drench us through;
Then if we lost our way what should we do?"

Laura turned cold as stone
To find her sister heard that cry alone,
That goblin cry,
"Come buy our fruits, come buy."
Must she then buy no more such dainty fruit?
Must she no more such succuous pasture find,
Gone deaf and blind?
Her tree of life drooped from the root:
She said not one word in her heart's sore ache;
But peering thro' the dimness, nought discerning,
Trudged home, her pitcher dripping all the way;
So crept to bed, and lay
Silent till Lizzie slept;
Then sat up in a passionate yearning,

And gnashed her teeth for baulked desire, and wept
As if her heart would break.

Day after day, night after night,
Laura kept watch in vain
In sullen silence of exceeding pain.
She never caught again the goblin cry:
"Come buy, come buy;"—
She never spied the goblin men
Hawking their fruits along the glen:
But when the noon waxed bright
Her hair grew thin and grey;
She dwindled, as the fair full moon doth turn
To swift decay and burn
Her fire away.

One day remembering her kernel-stone
She set it by a wall that faced the south;
Dewed it with tears, hoped for a root,
Watched for a waxing shoot,
But there came none;
It never saw the sun,
It never felt the trickling moisture run:
While with sunk eyes and faded mouth
She dreamed of melons, as a traveller sees
False waves in desert drouth
With shade of leaf-crowned trees,
And burns the thirstier in the sandful breeze.

She no more swept the house,
Tended the fowls or cows,
Fetched honey, kneaded cakes of wheat,
Brought water from the brook:
But sat down listless in the chimney-nook
And would not eat.

Tender Lizzie could not bear
To watch her sister's cankerous care
Yet not to share.
She night and morning
Caught the goblins' cry:
"Come buy our orchard fruits,
Come buy, come buy;"–
Beside the brook, along the glen,
She heard the tramp of goblin men,
The yoke and stir
Poor Laura could not hear;
Longed to buy fruit to comfort her,
But feared to pay too dear.
She thought of Jeanie in her grave,
Who should have been a bride;
But who for joys brides hope to have
Fell sick and died
In her gay prime,
In earliest winter time
With the first glazing rime,
With the first snow-fall of crisp winter time.

Till Laura dwindling
Seemed knocking at Death's door:
Then Lizzie weighed no more
Better and worse;
But put a silver penny in her purse,
Kissed Laura, crossed the heath with clumps of furze
At twilight, halted by the brook:
And for the first time in her life
Began to listen and look.

Laughed every goblin
When they spied her peeping:
Came towards her hobbling,
Flying, running, leaping,

Puffing and blowing,
Chuckling, clapping, crowing,
Clucking and gobbling,
Mopping and mowing,
Full of airs and graces,
Pulling wry faces,
Demure grimaces,
Cat-like and rat-like,
Ratel- and wombat-like,
Snail-paced in a hurry,
Parrot-voiced and whistler,
Helter skelter, hurry skurry,
Chattering like magpies,
Fluttering like pigeons,
Gliding like fishes,–
Hugged her and kissed her:
Squeezed and caressed her:
Stretched up their dishes,
Panniers, and plates:
"Look at our apples
Russet and dun,
Bob at our cherries,
Bite at our peaches,
Citrons and dates,
Grapes for the asking,
Pears red with basking
Out in the sun,
Plums on their twigs;
Pluck them and suck them,
Pomegranates, figs."–

"Good folk," said Lizzie,
Mindful of Jeanie:
"Give me much and many: –
Held out her apron,
Tossed them her penny.

"Nay, take a seat with us,
Honour and eat with us,"
They answered grinning:
"Our feast is but beginning.
Night yet is early,
Warm and dew-pearly,
Wakeful and starry:
Such fruits as these
No man can carry:
Half their bloom would fly,
Half their dew would dry,
Half their flavour would pass by.
Sit down and feast with us,
Be welcome guest with us,
Cheer you and rest with us."–
"Thank you," said Lizzie: "But one waits
At home alone for me:
So without further parleying,
If you will not sell me any
Of your fruits though much and many,
Give me back my silver penny
I tossed you for a fee."–
They began to scratch their pates,
No longer wagging, purring,
But visibly demurring,
Grunting and snarling.
One called her proud,
Cross-grained, uncivil;
Their tones waxed loud,
Their looks were evil.
Lashing their tails
They trod and hustled her,
Elbowed and jostled her,
Clawed with their nails,
Barking, mewing, hissing, mocking,
Tore her gown and soiled her stocking,

Twitched her hair out by the roots,
Stamped upon her tender feet,
Held her hands and squeezed their fruits
Against her mouth to make her eat.

White and golden Lizzie stood,
Like a lily in a flood,—
Like a rock of blue-veined stone
Lashed by tides obstreperously,—
Like a beacon left alone
In a hoary roaring sea,
Sending up a golden fire,—
Like a fruit-crowned orange-tree
White with blossoms honey-sweet
Sore beset by wasp and bee,—
Like a royal virgin town
Topped with gilded dome and spire
Close beleaguered by a fleet
Mad to tug her standard down.

One may lead a horse to water,
Twenty cannot make him drink.
Though the goblins cuffed and caught her,
Coaxed and fought her,
Bullied and besought her,
Scratched her, pinched her black as ink,
Kicked and knocked her,
Mauled and mocked her,
Lizzie uttered not a word;
Would not open lip from lip
Lest they should cram a mouthful in:
But laughed in heart to feel the drip
Of juice that syrupped all her face,
And lodged in dimples of her chin,
And streaked her neck which quaked like curd.
At last the evil people,

Worn out by her resistance,
Flung back her penny, kicked their fruit
Along whichever road they took,
Not leaving root or stone or shoot;
Some writhed into the ground,
Some dived into the brook
With ring and ripple,
Some scudded on the gale without a sound,
Some vanished in the distance.

In a smart, ache, tingle,
Lizzie went her way;
Knew not was it night or day;
Sprang up the bank, tore thro' the furze,
Threaded copse and dingle,
And heard her penny jingle
Bouncing in her purse,—
Its bounce was music to her ear.
She ran and ran
As if she feared some goblin man
Dogged her with gibe or curse
Or something worse:
But not one goblin scurried after,
Nor was she pricked by fear;
The kind heart made her windy-paced
That urged her home quite out of breath with haste
And inward laughter.

She cried, "Laura," up the garden,
"Did you miss me?
Come and kiss me.
Never mind my bruises,
Hug me, kiss me, suck my juices
Squeezed from goblin fruits for you,
Goblin pulp and goblin dew.
Eat me, drink me, love me;

Laura, make much of me;
For your sake I have braved the glen
And had to do with goblin merchant men."

Laura started from her chair,
Flung her arms up in the air,
Clutched her hair:
"Lizzie, Lizzie, have you tasted
For my sake the fruit forbidden?
Must your light like mine be hidden,
Your young life like mine be wasted,
Undone in mine undoing,
And ruined in my ruin,
Thirsty, cankered, goblin-ridden?"–
She clung about her sister,
Kissed and kissed and kissed her:
Tears once again
Refreshed her shrunken eyes,
Dropping like rain
After long sultry drouth;
Shaking with aguish fear, and pain,
She kissed and kissed her with a hungry mouth.

Her lips began to scorch,
That juice was wormwood to her tongue,
She loathed the feast:
Writhing as one possessed she leaped and sung,
Rent all her robe, and wrung
Her hands in lamentable haste,
And beat her breast.
Her locks streamed like the torch
Borne by a racer at full speed,
Or like the mane of horses in their flight,
Or like an eagle when she stems the light
Straight toward the sun,
Or like a caged thing freed,

Or like a flying flag when armies run.

Swift fire spread through her veins, knocked at her heart,
Met the fire smouldering there
And overbore its lesser flame;
She gorged on bitterness without a name:
Ah! fool, to choose such part
Of soul-consuming care!
Sense failed in the mortal strife:
Like the watch-tower of a town
Which an earthquake shatters down,
Like a lightning-stricken mast,
Like a wind-uprooted tree
Spun about,
Like a foam-topped waterspout
Cast down headlong in the sea,
She fell at last;
Pleasure past and anguish past,
Is it death or is it life?

Life out of death.
That night long Lizzie watched by her,
Counted her pulse's flagging stir,
Felt for her breath,
Held water to her lips, and cooled her face
With tears and fanning leaves:
But when the first birds chirped about their eaves,
And early reapers plodded to the place
Of golden sheaves,
And dew-wet grass
Bowed in the morning winds so brisk to pass,
And new buds with new day
Opened of cup-like lilies on the stream,
Laura awoke as from a dream,
Laughed in the innocent old way,
Hugged Lizzie but not twice or thrice;

Her gleaming locks showed not one thread of grey,
Her breath was sweet as May
And light danced in her eyes.

Days, weeks, months, years
Afterwards, when both were wives
With children of their own;
Their mother-hearts beset with fears,
Their lives bound up in tender lives;
Laura would call the little ones
And tell them of her early prime,
Those pleasant days long gone
Of not-returning time:
Would talk about the haunted glen,
The wicked, quaint fruit-merchant men,
Their fruits like honey to the throat
But poison in the blood;
(Men sell not such in any town):
Would tell them how her sister stood
In deadly peril to do her good,
And win the fiery antidote:
Then joining hands to little hands
Would bid them cling together,
"For there is no friend like a sister
In calm or stormy weather;
To cheer one on the tedious way,
To fetch one if one goes astray,
To lift one if one totters down,
To strengthen whilst one stands."

QUESTIONS

1. The poem begins: "Morning and evening/ Maids heard
   the goblins cry". "Maids" means "girls/women" (not
   housemaids!), so why don't men hear them? Where are

the men in this poem? Are men represented by the goblins? if so, what is Rossetti saying about the relationship between men and women?

2. The fruit is often taken as a reference to the "forbidden fruit" on the "tree of the knowledge of good and evil" in the Garden of Eden (see Genesis 2:16–17). Is this poem therefore a reworking of that story?

3. Is it Laura's fault that she eats the "forbidden fruit"? Consider how she is warned by her sister, her curiosity, and the fact that Lizzie resists. Relate this question to present day problems of alcohol and drug addiction.

4. Some critics have seen lesbian overtones in the lines:

   - Crouching close together
   - In the cooling weather,
   - With clasping arms and cautioning lips,
   - With tingling cheeks and finger tips.
   - "Lie close," Laura said.

   There are even stronger passages later on. Read these, and say whether you agree.

5. Critics have also seen sexual references in the poem and suggest that the "forbidden fruit" is sex. Read from: "Then sucked their fruit globes fair or red" to "She sucked until her lips were sore" and find other passages of the same type (see, for example, the passage beginning "Hug me, kiss me, suck my juices"), then discuss the idea.

6. Some critics (Marxist literary critics) have said that the poem is a critique of capitalism with its emphasis on

buying and selling, and the damage that does to people. Investigate the evidence for this idea.

7. Some critics have seen echoes of Jesus Christ in the self-sacrifice of Lizzie, especially in the line: "Eat me, drink me, love me", which is exactly what Christians are asked to do (though in different words) in the Communion Service. Critics often term this "the Eucharistic passage". What other religious themes can be found in this poem?

8. Examine closely the effects of sound in the poem: alliteration, assonance, consonance, onomatopoeia, sibilance, rhyme and rhythm.

9. The stated moral of the poem is "there is no friend like a sister". Do you think this is an effective moral for the whole poem? What other morals could be drawn from it?

10. Feminist critics see this poem as a celebration of women's power, especially with the support of the "sisterhood". How far do you agree with this interpretation?

11. Rossetti claimed that the poem was not meant for children. However, in public Rossetti often stated that the poem was intended for children, and went on to write many children's poems. In your opinion, is this a children's poem, a poem for adults, or can it work on both levels?

COMMENTARY

It is a tribute to the richness of this poem that, like Shakespeare's plays, many interpretations are possible, some of them so off the wall that it makes you wonder how anybody could take them seriously! Here is a list:

a celebration of homosexual love
a celebration of sisterly love
a complaint about the lack of fresh fruit in Victorian England
a critique of capitalism
a critique of the rise of advertising in Victorian England
a critique of Victorian sexual values
a fairy tale for children
a reworking of the Garden of Eden story
a sexual fantasy
an allegory of substance addiction
an allegory of Christ's sacrifice
an anti-Semitic rant
an expression of Rossetti's feminism

The poem certainly works at both child and adult level. A child's innocence would not see any sexual connotations in any of the descriptions, but would enjoy them at a literal level as referring only to the enjoyment of delicious fruit. The touching and kissing of the sisters for them is not sexual, but merely sisterly. However, it is difficult for any adult to read the poem without noticing the sexual connotations. These were probably not intentional on Rossetti's part. As a devout High Church Christian, she would be horrified at what some people have read into the poem. The sexual connotations may be there, nevertheless (though this is not the place to get into reader-response theory – you'll have to wait for uni for that!). They may be a by-product of sexual sublimation or repression. Here is how Weor (2006) described it:

Sublimation is the transference of sexual energy, or libido, into a physical act or a different emotion in order to avoid confrontation with the sexual urge, which is itself contrary to the individual's belief or ascribed religious belief.

Freud's theory, in the words of Bannister, describes the human personality as

...basically a battlefield. He is a dark-cellar in which a well-bred spinster lady (the superego) and a sex-crazed monkey (the id) are forever engaged in mortal combat, the struggle being refereed by a rather nervous bank clerk (the ego).

Rossetti had three love affairs (we don't know how involved she became, but a typical Victorian middle class courtship was a fairly chaste matter) but never married. She expresses regret for what she has missed in her poem *A Daughter of Eve*, so no doubt, she had strong sexual feelings under the surface which may have come out unconsciously in *Goblin Market*. Here is some of the evidence:

The first description of Laura eating the fruit is that she: "sucked their fruit globes fair or red". The female breast is often compared to fruit: melons, pomegraates (in Persian Literature) apples. Even the colours suggest the breast (occidental ones, at any rate): fair (pale skin), red (nipples). Sucking is of course something that both babies and lovers do to breasts. Later on, in another highly erotic scene, Lizzie says: "Hug me, kiss me, suck my juices". Hugging and kissing, as well as gestures of bonding between family members, are sexual. Sucking juices... well, in a book aimed at students who may not yet have achieved their majority, the less said, the better. But is this lesbian sex? Scenes like the following certainly suggest it:

Lizzie veiled her blushes:

> Crouching close together
> In the cooling weather,
> With clasping arms and cautioning lips,
> With tingling cheeks and finger tips.
> "Lie close," Laura said.

Not to mention, later in the poem:

> Eat me, drink me, love me;
> Laura, make much of me.

There are several other such passages. If there are lesbian overtones in the poem, they certainly came from the very deepest of repressed feelings. Rossetti, who knew her Bible inside out would have known that such love is forbidden in the Bible (e.g., Romans 1:26-27).

All these subconscious references to sexuality, both hetero- and homo-sexual are rationalised by Rossetti in the moral of her poem "there is no friend like a sister".

Another valid interpretation of the poem, which exists side by side with the sexual interpretation, is that it is a reworking of the Garden of Eden story as it contains a specific reference to forbidden fruit, and vividly portrays temptation (though the word is use nowhere in the text). The Fall of Man is seen by Christians as being redeemed by Christ's self sacrifice on the cross (Romans 5:12-21). Similarly, Lizzie saves Laura by risking her life to get some Goblin fruit for her.

The link with the theme of sexuality is as follows: Sex really was a forbidden fruit in Victorian times, particularly for women because of the "double standard". A good Victorian woman was expected to come to her marriage bed as a virgin, and when she had sex, not to enjoy it, but to "lie back and think of England" (The well-known phrase originated a little later than the Victorian period when, in 1912, Lady Hillingdon wrote in her journal: "When I hear his steps outside my door I lie down on my bed, open my legs and think of England.")

The final question to consider is: is this a children's poem, a poem for adults, or is it suitable for both? The answer is simply to look at the two versions of the poem in this book. *Goblin Market (Lite)* is edited to make it shorter, not to remove any sexual connotations, but the questions and commentaries which follow omit these themes. It can be seen that the poem is fully enjoyable and understandable at a simpler level as a fairy story for children. That there is another level of sophisticated adult analysis is obvious from this commentary.

Goblin Market (Lite)

This version of Goblin Market has been reduced to one third of the length of the original for study purposes, with short summaries to bridge the gaps. It has been divided into four parts. Questions and Commentaries follow each part.

PART 1

Morning and evening
Maids heard the goblins cry:
"Come buy our orchard fruits,
Come buy, come buy:
Apples and quinces,
Lemons and oranges,
Plump unpecked cherries,
Melons and raspberries,
Bloom-down-cheeked peaches,
Swart-headed mulberries,
Wild free-born cranberries,
Crabapples, dewberries,
Pineapples, blackberries,
Apricots, strawberries; –
All ripe together
In summer weather…

15 lines of description are omitted here.

Evening by evening
Among the brookside rushes,
Laura bowed her head to hear,
Lizzie veiled her blushes:
Crouching close together
In the cooling weather,

With clasping arms and cautioning lips,
With tingling cheeks and finger tips.
"Lie close," Laura said,
Pricking up her golden head:
"We must not look at goblin men,
We must not buy their fruits:
Who knows upon what soil they fed
Their hungry thirsty roots?"
"Come buy," call the goblins
Hobbling down the glen.
"Oh," cried Lizzie, "Laura, Laura,
You should not peep at goblin men."
"No," said Lizzie; "No, no, no;
Their offers should not charm us,
Their evil gifts would harm us."
She thrust a dimpled finger
In each ear, shut eyes and ran:
Curious Laura chose to linger
Wondering at each merchant man.
One had a cat's face,
One whisked a tail,
One tramped at a rat's pace,
One crawled like a snail,
One like a wombat prowled obtuse and furry,
One like a ratel tumbled hurry skurry.
She heard a voice like voice of doves
Cooing all together:
They sounded kind and full of loves
In the beautiful weather.

Laura stretched her gleaming neck
Like a rush-embedded swan,
Like a lily from the beck,
Like a moonlit poplar branch,
Like a vessel at the launch
When its last restraint is gone...

152 lines are omitted here. In these lines there is more description of the goblins and of Laura's temptation.

"Come buy, come buy," was still their cry.
Laura stared but did not stir,
Longed but had no money:
One parrot-voiced and jolly
Cried "Pretty Goblin" still for "Pretty Polly;"–
One whistled like a bird.

- brook – a dialect word for stream
- ratel – honey badger (Mellivora capensis)
- beck – a different dialect word for stream

QUESTIONS

1. Count how many different fruits are for sale. Make list of adjectives used to describe the fruits. What is the total effect of this?

2. What warning does Lizzie give to Laura? What reasons does she give? What was Laura's reaction?

3. The goblins are described using animal references. Make a list of the animals mentioned.

4. Make list of the adjectives and similes used to describe the goblins.

5. What is the effect of the anaphora in this description of the goblins?

6. How is Rossetti's description of the goblins similar or different to descriptions of goblins in folk tale and fantasy writing?

7. What is the effect of the anaphora of "Like a…"

8. What is ironic (in view of what happens later) about the line "They sounded kind and full of loves"?

9. What do the first three similes tell us about Laura?

10. What point is being made in the last simile?

11. Why is Laura unable to buy the fruit?

12. Analyse the verse form of this extract and write a description of it.

COMMENTARY

The poem begins with a description of the goblins' cry to come and buy their fruit. The verse form is irregular, often using couplets or a b a b rhymes, but other patterns are also used. The metre is also irregular, with varying line lengths and stress patterns. This allows the author great flexibility which gives room for creativity. Of all Rossetti's poems, this has the freest verse form and is also the most imaginative.

The description of the goblins' fruit is made to sound as tempting as possible. Not only is there a very wide range: sixteen kinds are mentioned initially (more later), but they are described with a range of powerful adjectives: "unpecked", "bloom-down-cheeked", "free-born", "ripe".

Two sisters, Laura and Lizzie, hear the goblins' cry. Laura listens intently, but Lizzie warns her, supporting her words of warning with these arguments: "who knows upon what soil they fed/ Their hungry thirsty roots?" and "Their offers should not charm us,/ Their evil gifts would harm us."

Next we have a description of the goblins in a long passage of anaphora in which each line begins with the word "one". Each line includes an animal reference, some of them in the form of a simile. This emphasises their animal-like nature; they are not the deformed humans of folk or fantasy literature. It also emphasises their great variety of appearance and movement. In view of what happens later in the poem, it is ironic that "They sounded kind and full of loves" – this, of course, is just a trick to lure their victim. One critic commented that the description of the goblins is "Hebraic" and that therefore the poem has an anti-Semitic theme. However, such off-the-wall interpretations should be taken with a pinch of salt!

Anaphora is used again, with a series of similes, to describe Laura's predicament: "Like a rush-embedded swan" tells us that she is trapped among the goblins by her desire for the fruit. The other similes are descriptions of her "stretched" neck. "Streched" because she is peering eagerly at the fruit. The final simile is the most powerful, emphasising that she cannot resist the temptation of the fruit.

This extract ends with Laura longing for the fruit but being unable to buy any because she has no money, followed by a humorous description of a goblin like a parrot.

PART 2

Part 2 follows straight on from Part 1 in the original.

But sweet-tooth Laura spoke in haste:
"Good folk, I have no coin."
To take were to purloin:
I have no copper in my purse,
I have no silver either,
And all my gold is on the furze
That shakes in windy weather
Above the rusty heather."
"You have much gold upon your head,"
They answered all together:
"Buy from us with a golden curl."
She clipped a precious golden lock,
She dropped a tear more rare than pearl,
Then sucked their fruit globes fair or red:
Sweeter than honey from the rock,
Stronger than man-rejoicing wine,
Clearer than water flowed that juice;
She never tasted such before,
How could it cloy with length of use?
She sucked and sucked and sucked the more
Fruits which that unknown orchard bore;
She sucked until her lips were sore;
Then flung the emptied rinds away
But gathered up one kernel-stone,
And knew not was it night or day
And she turned home alone.

Lizzie met her at the gate
Full of wise upbraidings:
"Dear, you should not stay so late,
Twilight is not good, for maidens
Should not loiter in the glen

In the haunts of goblin men.
Do you not remember Jeanie,
How she met them in the moonlight,
Took their gifts both choice and many,
Ate their fruits and wore their flowers
Plucked from bowers
Where summer ripens at all hours?
But ever in the noonlight
She pined and pined away;
Sought them by night and day,
Found them no more but dwindled and grew grey;
Then fell with the first snow,
While to this day no grass will grow
Where she lies low:
I planted daisies there a year ago
That never blow.
You should not loiter so."
"Nay, hush," said Laura:
"Nay, hush, my sister:
I ate and ate my fill,
Yet my mouth waters still;
Tomorrow night I will buy more."

- purloin – steal
- furze – the genus Ulex, of the legume family, having yellow flowers. It is a crop used for animal fodder.

QUESTIONS

1. Explain the metaphor in the line: "all my gold is on the furze".

2. Explain the metaphor in the line: "You have much gold upon your head"

3. Consider the lines: "She clipped a precious golden lock,/ She dropped a tear more rare than pearl". How can a lock of her hair be "precious" and a tear "more rare than pearl"? What is the author trying to say here?

4. Re-read from "Then sucked..." to "lips were sore" and answer the following questions: How many times is the word "sucked" used? Which line emphasises how much she sucked?

5. What figures of speech are used to emphasise the taste of the fruit? Explain each one fully.

6. What does the line "[she] knew not was it night or day" tell us about her physical state after gorging on the fruit?

7. In your own words, retell the story of Jeanie. Why does Lizzie tell her sister this story?

8. Re-read the last three lines and explain in your own words what is strange about the physical feeling that Laura is left with.

COMMENTARY

The second extract begins with Laura saying that she has no money to pay for the fruit. Note how the money metals escalate through three lines from copper to gold. But the gold she refers to is "on the furze". From this, we learn that Laura and Lizzie make their living by harvesting furze (which they would sell for animal fodder). The goblins take up the idea of gold and ask for a lock of her blonde hair. This is more valuable to them as it will give them power over her by a kind of "sympathetic magic". The next two lines: "She clipped a precious golden lock,/ She dropped a tear more rare than pearl" emphasise the value of the hair (and her tear): these things are part of her being, and thus more "precious" than any material object, such as money, gold or pearls, can be.

The lines that follow emphasise Laura's delight in tasting the fruits. Their taste is described in the simile "sweeter than honey". The comparative "Stronger than man-rejoicing wine", shows that the fruit is more intoxicating than alcohol. The repetition of the word "suck" (five times) suggests that she is like an addict in the intensity of her "fix". The last two lines of the strophe show that she is so intoxicated that she has lost all sense of time.

Her sister meets her and tells her off, using the story of Jeanie to emphasise her point. Jeanie also ate the goblin fruit and as a consequence, pined away and died. No grass will grow on her grave. Laura replies by expressing her anxiety that though she ate her fill she still longs for more.

PART 3

Laura tries to find the goblins again, but can no longer hear their cries and so cannot find them. She grows thin and grey with pining. Lizzie is so worried about her that she goes to buy some goblin fruit for her.

Laughed every goblin
When they spied her peeping:
Come towards her hobbling,
Flying, running, leaping,
Puffing and blowing,
Chuckling, clapping, crowing,
Clucking and gobbling,
Mopping and mowing,
Full of airs and graces,
Pulling wry faces,
Demure grimaces,
Cat-like and rat-like,
Ratel- and wombat-like,
Snail-paced in a hurry,
Parrot-voiced and whistler,
Helter skelter, hurry skurry,
Chattering like magpies,
Fluttering like pigeons,
Gliding like fishes, –
Hugged her and kissed her,
Squeezed and caressed her:
Stretched up their dishes,
Panniers and plates:
"Look at our apples
Russet and dun,
Bob at our cherries,
Bite at our peaches,
Citrons and dates,
Grapes for the asking,

Pears red with basking
Out in the sun,
Plums on their twigs;
Pluck them and suck them,
Pomegranates, figs.
"Good folk," said Lizzie,
Mindful of Jeanie:
"Give me much and many,"
Held out her apron,
Tossed them her penny.

QUESTIONS

1. In this extract, many gerunds (the –*ing* form of the verb) are used to describe the goblins. How many gerunds can you count? List and comment on unusual and interesting ones.

2. Compound adjectives (e.g, cat-like) are used to emphasise their animal appearance and behaviour. Explain in one in detail and say what over effect they have.

3. Identify some words and phrases that show that the goblins are delighted to see Lizzie. What is the reason for their delight?

4. List the action verbs that the goblins use to tempt Lizzie.

5. Why is Lizzie "mindful of Jeanie" when she asks for "much and many"?

6. Why does she want to pay with money?

COMMENTARY

In the 199 lines that have been omitted in this version, Laura tries to find the goblins again, but can no longer hear their cries and so cannot find them. She grows thin and grey with pining. Lizzie is worried about her. She "longed to buy fruit to comfort her,/ But feared to pay too dear." However, because of her love for her sister, she overcomes her fear and goes to buy some goblin fruit for her.

The goblins are delighted when they see her coming, thinking, no doubt, that here was another victim. Rossetti portrays this very skilfully with a series of gerunds. The first four describe their eager movements towards her. The next seven describes the sounds they make, mainly gloating sounds as they sense an easy victory. The next two, their gestures of false deference. This is followed by a second extended description of the goblins, once again emphasising their animal qualities. They make much of her in order to win her over: "Hugged her and kissed her,/ Squeezed and caressed her" and try to tempt her with their fruit, of which more varieties are mentioned. Lizzie asks for a lot of them, but in doing so, she is, of course, "mindful of Jeanie" – in other words, she is determined to pay with money and not to eat the fruit herself.

PART 4

The goblins try to make Lizzie eat their fruit by pushing it into her face, but she resists temptation and keeps her mouth firmly shut. However, the juice and pulp goes all over her face. When she gets home, she calls a welcome to Laura:

She cried, "Laura," up the garden,
"Did you miss me?
Come and kiss me.
Never mind my bruises,
Hug me, kiss me, suck my juices
Squeezed from goblin fruits for you,
Goblin pulp and goblin dew.
Eat me, drink me, love me;
Laura, make much of me;
For your sake I have braved the glen
And had to do with goblin merchant men."

Laura started from her chair,
Flung her arms up in the air,
Clutched her hair:
"Lizzie, Lizzie, have you tasted
For my sake the fruit forbidden?
Must your light like mine be hidden,
Your young life like mine be wasted,
Undone in mine undoing,
And ruined in my ruin,
Thirsty, cankered, goblin-ridden?"–
She clung about her sister,
Kissed and kissed and kissed her:
Tears once again
Refreshed her shrunken eyes,
Dropping like rain
After long sultry drouth;
Shaking with aguish fear, and pain,

She kissed and kissed her with a hungry mouth.

Her lips began to scorch,
That juice was wormwood to her tongue,
She loathed the feast:
Writhing as one possessed she leaped and sung,
Rent all her robe, and wrung
Her hands in lamentable haste,
And beat her breast.
Her locks streamed like the torch
Borne by a racer at full speed,
Or like the mane of horses in their flight,
Or like an eagle when she stems the light
Straight toward the sun,
Or like a caged thing freed,
Or like a flying flag when armies run.

Swift fire spread through her veins, knocked at her heart,
Met the fire smouldering there
And overbore its lesser flame;
She gorged on bitterness without a name:
Ah! fool, to choose such part
Of soul-consuming care!
Sense failed in the mortal strife:
Like the watch-tower of a town
Which an earthquake shatters down,
Like a lightning-stricken mast,
Like a wind-uprooted tree
Spun about,
Like a foam-topped waterspout
Cast down headlong in the sea,
She fell at last;
Pleasure past and anguish past,
Is it death or is it life?

Laura suffers a night of severe illness during which Lizzie does everything she can to save her. The next morning Laura is well again:

> Her gleaming locks showed not one thread of grey,
> Her breath was sweet as May
> And light danced in her eyes.

The poem ends, years later, with Laura telling her children about what happened.

- wormwood – The word occurs frequently in the Bible, and generally in a metaphorical sense. In (Jeremiah 9:15; 23:15; Lamentations 3:15; Lamentations 3:19). Wormwood is symbolical of bitter calamity and sorrow

QUESTIONS

1. Pick out some words and phrases that show Lizzie has risked sacrificing herself to save her sister.

2. What language does Laura use to describe her physical state?

3. What figure of speech is used to describe Laura's tears and why is it so powerful?

4. Comment on the repetition of the word "kiss" in the first two strophes of the extract.

5. Re-read from "Her lips…" to "…her breast". What metaphorical language is used to describe Laura's fever in these lines?

6. Re-read from "Her locks…" to "…armies run". How is

anaphora used in these lines? Explain the effect of each simile in describing Laura's fever."

7. What metaphorical language is used in the first part of the final strophe (up to "soul-consuming care!") to describe Laura's fever?

8. The anaphora of similes continues in the final strophe of the extract. Explain each simile and say why they are so effective in describing a life-threatening fever.

9. What figurative language is used in the final three lines to show that Laura is well again?

COMMENTARY

In the 99 lines that are omitted in this version, the goblins try to make Lizzie their fruit by pushing it into her face, but she resists temptation and keeps her mouth firmly shut. The juice, however, goes all over her face. When she gets home, she calls a welcome to Laura and invites her to "suck my juices/ Squeezed from goblin fruits for you". Laura replies with an expression of surprise at the sacrifice that her sister has made to save her: "Lizzie, Lizzie, have you tasted/ For my sake the fruit forbidden?". Note the Biblical allusion (to Genesis 2:16–17) in the phrase "fruit forbidden". Laura then expresses her fear that her life might also be "wasted", or in the more vivid expression that follows: "Thirsty, cankered, goblin-ridden?" They kiss (the word is repeated five times). It is both a kiss of love, and for Laura of revival as she swallows the juice of the goblin fruit. Note the reference to tears. Her last tear was shed when she paid for the goblin fruit with a lock of her hair. She has not been able to cry since, despite her suffering, but now:

Tears once again
Refreshed her shrunken eyes,
Dropping like rain
After long sultry drouth.

A fever follows, its heat emphasised by the word "scorch" and its psychological effect by the word "wormwood", a Biblical term which meant bitterness and sorrow. Laura's physical restlessness is vividly described by a list of vivid similes, for example, Particularly by the simile "as one possessed". After a few lines of vivid description, there are five more vivid similes in an anaphoric pattern. This piling up of description is a noteworthy feature of Rossetti's technique throughout this poem.

The next strophe continues in the same vein with four more vivid similes in the same anaphoric pattern. The similes get stronger and stronger as the crisis of Laura's fever approaches: "earthquake", "lightening", "cast down". At the end of the strophe her life hangs in the balance.

The 16 lines that are omitted describe how Lizzie watched over Laura, and how she gradually revives. The next three lines show that Laura has made a complete recovery, especially in the metaphor "light danced". This shows that she is happy again, so it is a psychological as well as a physical recovery.

In the final 25 lines, the poem ends, years later, with Laura telling her children about what happened, and leading up to the "moral" of the tale: "there is no friend like a sister".

The next step is to re-read the full version of the poem and to work through the more advanced questions that follow.

Song: When I Am Dead, My Dearest

When I am dead, my dearest,
Sing no sad songs for me;
Plant thou no roses at my head,
Nor shady cypress tree:
Be the green grass above me
With showers and dewdrops wet;
And if thou wilt, remember,
And if thou wilt, forget.

I shall not see the shadows,
I shall not feel the rain;
I shall not hear the nightingale
Sing on, as if in pain:
And dreaming through the twilight
That doth not rise nor set,
Haply I may remember,
And haply may forget.

- haply – perhaps

QUESTIONS

1. Explain the poem's message in simple words. What is the difference in focus between stanza one and stanza two?

2. What are the usual connotations of the song of a nightingale? How does Rossetti change this in this poem?

3. How would you describe the tone of this poem? Consider the words: pessimistic, nihilistic, indifferent, detached.

4. In what sense is the tone of this poem, and ideas expressed, inconsistent with the views a devout Christian would hold?

5. Where is anaphora used in the poem and what is its effect?

6. Describe the verse form of the poem. In what sense is it song-like?

7. Comment on the use of alliteration in the poem.

8. Compare and contrast the poem with *Remember.*

9. Compare the picture of the afterlife in the poem with that presented in *Paradise: in a Dream.*

COMMENTARY

This poem was written in 1848 and may refer to one of her earlier periods of illness. She may also have been experiencing one of her periods of religious doubt, and this may account for the detached, almost nihilistic tone of the poem, which contains no hint of Christ's promise of a glorious afterlife, such as she describes in *Paradise: in a Dream.*

The verse form of the poem is based on ballad form, with two ballad form stanzas put together in one stanza. This gives it the rhythmical flow of a ballad, and together with the anaphora gives the poem a song-like quality. The simplicity of the form provides an interesting counterpoint to the complexity of the mood expressed.

In the first stanza, she is telling her "dearest" not to perform the usual memorials, and that he may or may not remember her, just as he wishes. This is similar, but subtly different to the message in *Remember*, where she wishes her to spare her loved ones the grief that may be caused by remembering her.

The second stanza, through a haunting anaphora, lists some of the things she will miss when she is dead (no mention here of a joyous afterlife). The third item, the song of the nightingale, involves a powerful reversal of the usual connotations, which can be seen in this extract from Keats' *Ode to a Nightingale*:

Tis not through envy of thy happy lot,
  But being too happy in thine happiness,–
    That thou, light-winged Dryad of the trees,
      In some melodious plot
    Of beechen green, and shadows numberless,
      Singest of summer in full-throated ease.

However, as Keats' ode progresses we see that the nightingale's song also has darker connotations:

Darkling I listen; and, for many a time
  I have been half in love with easeful Death…

Perhaps Keats' ode was in Rossetti's thoughts when she wrote these lines. However we interpret them, the mood is negative, as is the reference to "the twilight That doth not rise nor set" which follows. This is how many earlier religions saw life after death, as a perpetual twilight – very different from the Christian heaven, which is seen as a better, fuller life, as we can see from several Biblical descriptions like this one from *Revelation*:

And the city had no need of the sun, neither of the moon, to shine in it: for the glory of God did lighten it, and the Lamb [is] the light thereof. (Revelation 21:23)

The last lines of the poem parallel the last lines of the first stanza in which she expresses her indifference and detachment.

In the Bleak Mid-Winter

In the bleak mid-winter
Frosty wind made moan,
Earth stood hard as iron,
Water like a stone;
Snow had fallen, snow on snow,
Snow on snow,
In the bleak mid-winter
Long ago.

Our God, Heaven cannot hold Him
Nor earth sustain;
Heaven and earth shall flee away
When He comes to reign:
In the bleak mid-winter
A stable-place sufficed
The Lord God Almighty,
Jesus Christ.

Enough for Him, whom cherubim
Worship night and day,
A breastful of milk,
And a mangerful of hay;
Enough for Him, whom angels
Fall down before,
The ox and ass and camel
Which adore.

Angels and archangels
May have gathered there,
Cherubim and seraphim
Thronged the air –
But only His mother

In her maiden bliss
Worshipped the Beloved
With a kiss.

What can I give Him,
Poor as I am?
If I were a shepherd
I would bring a lamb;
If I were a wise man
I would do my part;
Yet what I can, I give Him -
Give my heart.

- bleak – cold, desolate, miserable

- Cherubim and Seraphim – these are powerful
  heavenly beings with four faces and four wings,
  whose job is to sing continually: "Holy, holy, holy
  is the Lord God Almighty."

QUESTIONS

1. Describe the verse form of the poem.

2. What is the effect of the emphasis on cold in stanzas
   one and two?

3. How do the similes in the first stanza emphasise the
   description of a "bleak midwinter"?

4. How is repetition used in the first stanza?

5. Much of the poetic power of the poem is based on
   antithesis; the contrast between what is great, powerful,
   wealthy, with what is humble, ordinary and poor.

Describe in your own words this antithesis in each stanza from two to four.

6. Explain the metaphor "give my heart". Why is this a much better gift than a lamb or the gifts of the wise men (gold, frankincense and myrrh)?

7. Explain the phrase "maiden bliss".

8. What change of focus is there in the last stanza?

9. Compare and contrast with her poem, *Love Came Down at Christmas*.

Love came down at Christmas,
Love all lovely, Love Divine,
Love was born at Christmas,
Star and Angels gave the sign.

Worship we the Godhead,
Love Incarnate, Love Divine,
Worship we our Jesus,
But wherewith for sacred sign?

Love shall be our token,
Love be yours and love be mine,
Love to God and all men,
Love for plea and gift and sign.

COMMENTARY

This poems draws on Victorian Britain's version of the Nativity. The birth stories are given in the Gospels of Matthew and Luke. They do not mention the time of year that Jesus was born, and even in January it is not that cold in Palestine (5°C to 10°C average). Snow can fall, but it is infrequent and never more than a few centimetres. Further, the theology of "Heaven cannot hold Him" and "Heaven and earth shall flee away/ When He comes to reign" is questionable (see article in Wikipedia). However, this is not a theological treatise it is a poem, and a very powerful one.

The poem begins by evoking, through powerful similes, a sense of intense cold. In the second stanza, we are told that, despite the cold, only a stable was available. This emphasizes one of the key messages of Christianity, that God identifies with the poor. This stanza also includes a powerful antithesis. God is so great that "heaven cannot hold Him Nor earth sustain" yet he chose a humble stable when he came among us as Jesus.

The third stanza continues the use of antithesis. In this case, between cherubim and seraphim who "worship night and day", and the humble and human "breastful of milk" (no formula milk powders in 1st century Palestine!).

The antithesis in the fourth stanza is even more powerful and moving. All the hosts of heaven (angels, archangels, cherubim and seraphim) are contrasted with his mother, and her humble, human kiss is seen as worth far more than the worship of the angel hosts.

There is a shift of perspective in the last stanza as Rossetti considers what she can give to Christ. She refers to the gifts mentioned in the traditional narrative, and concludes that, as she has nothing, she can only give her heart, and yet this is the most precious gift anyone can give, 'heart' being symbolic of one's love and devotion.

Part of the power of the poem lies in its simplicity. The verse form is an eight-line stanza, consisting mainly of trimeters (three-stress lines) and ending with a dimeter (a two-stress line). The rhyme scheme is simple and ballad-like as only alternate lines rhyme. The simple verse form can also be described as song-like, and indeed the poem has been given several musical settings, the most popular being settings by Gustav Holst (1906) and Harold Darke (1909).

It is interesting to compare this poem to *Love came down at Christmas*, which has also been set to music and become a popular Christmas carol. This poem is shorter and simpler, but makes its impact through the key word, the oft-repeated "love".

A Birthday

My heart is like a singing bird
Whose nest is in a watered shoot;
My heart is like an apple-tree
Whose boughs are bent with thick-set fruit;
My heart is like a rainbow shell
That paddles in a halcyon sea;
My heart is gladder than all these,
Because my love is come to me.

Raise me a dais of silk and down;
Hang it with vair and purple dyes;
Carve it in doves and pomegranates,
And peacocks with a hundred eyes;
Work it in gold and silver grapes,
In leaves and silver fleurs-de-lys;
Because the birthday of my life
Is come, my love is come to me.

- halcyon – calm, peaceful
- dais – raised platform
- vair – greyish blue (a fur in heraldry)
- fleurs-de-lys – a heraldic device resembling three petals of an iris

QUESTIONS

1. Explain the series of extended similes in the first stanza. What is compared to what, and what is the effect of the comparison. What does the extension (viz., the second, fourth and sixth lines) add to the power of the simile?

2. Stanza two follows the pattern of the stanza one, but with imperatives. What is the poet asking her friends to do? What would be the overall effect of the decoration?

3. What is the reason for this lavish decoration?

4. Explain the phrase "birthday of my life". How is it different from an ordinary birthday?

5. Is it possible to relate this poem to her biography, given that she never married any of her suitors? Or is the character in the poem an imagined persona?

6. Find three words to describe the tone of the poem.

7. Write down the rhyme scheme of the poem, and explain it.

8. What is the metrical pattern of each line?

COMMENTARY

This is a highly symmetrical poem consisting of two stanzas rhymed like two ballad-form stanzas (a b c b d e f e) but in tetrameter throughout. Anaphora adds to the symmetry: three extended similes in stanza one and three imperatives in stanza two. The last phrase of each stanza forms a refrain.

The first stanza expresses great joy through the series of extended similes. Joy symbolized by a singing bird, and the extension of the simile suggesting growth, perhaps alluding to the personal growth that results from love. The force of the second simile is in its extension "Whose boughs are bent with thick-set fruit" which suggests abundance and fertility. The third simile has a metaphor within it – the shell is the shape of the rainbow over the sea. "Halcyon" means that the sea is calm and peaceful, but there is may also be an allusion to the use of the word by classical writers to describe a mythical bird in a nest floating on sea, charming the wind and waves into calm. The last two lines of the stanza give the reason for all this joy: "Because my love is come to me."

The second stanza continues the pattern with a series of imperatives, which are, in effect, instructions for the decorations of a birthday party. The descriptions are richly exotic in colours, precious metals, beautiful birds and heraldic ornaments ("vair", "fleurs-de-lys") which give a formal magnificence to the decorations. Once again, the reason for this extravagant decoration is given in the last two lines: "Because the birthday of my life/ Is come, my love is come to me." "Birthday of my life" is a powerful metaphor, because, while a birthday is a special event that comes once a year, falling love comes once in a lifetime (or at least, not very often).

It is interesting to consider if there is an autobiographical element in the poem, as it may recall the happy time when one of her suitors first declared his love.

Jessie Cameron

"Jessie, Jessie Cameron,
  Hear me but this once," quoth he.
"Good luck go with you, neighbour's son,
  But I'm no mate for you," quoth she.
Day was verging toward the night
  There beside the moaning sea,
Dimness overtook the light
  There where the breakers be.
"O Jessie, Jessie Cameron,
  I have loved you long and true."–
"Good luck go with you, neighbour's son,
  But I'm no mate for you."

She was a careless, fearless girl,
  And made her answer plain,
Outspoken she to earl or churl,
  Kindhearted in the main,
But somewhat heedless with her tongue,
  And apt at causing pain;
A mirthful maiden she and young,
  Most fair for bliss or bane.
"Oh, long ago I told you so,
  I tell you so to-day:
Go you your way, and let me go
  Just my own free way."

The sea swept in with moan and foam,
  Quickening the stretch of sand;
They stood almost in sight of home;
  He strove to take her hand.
"Oh, can't you take your answer then,
  And won't you understand?

For me you're not the man of men,
  I've other plans are planned.
You're good for Madge, or good for Cis,
  Or good for Kate, may be:
But what's to me the good of this
  While you're not good for me?"

They stood together on the beach,
  They two alone,
And louder waxed his urgent speech,
  His patience almost gone:
"Oh, say but one kind word to me,
  Jessie, Jessie Cameron."–
"I'd be too proud to beg," quoth she,
  And pride was in her tone.
And pride was in her lifted head,
  And in her angry eye
And in her foot, which might have fled,
  But would not fly.

Some say that he had gipsy blood;
  That in his heart was guile:
Yet he had gone through fire and flood
  Only to win her smile.
Some say his grandam was a witch,
  A black witch from beyond the Nile,
Who kept an image in a niche
  And talked with it the while.
And by her hut far down the lane
  Some say they would not pass at night,
Lest they should hear an unked strain
  Or see an unked sight.

Alas, for Jessie Cameron!–
  The sea crept moaning, moaning nigher:
She should have hastened to begone,–

The sea swept higher, breaking by her:
She should have hastened to her home
  While yet the west was flushed with fire,
But now her feet are in the foam,
  The sea-foam, sweeping higher.
O mother, linger at your door,
  And light your lamp to make it plain,
But Jessie she comes home no more,
  No more again.

They stood together on the strand,
  They only, each by each;
Home, her home, was close at hand,
  Utterly out of reach.
Her mother in the chimney nook
  Heard a startled sea-gull screech,
But never turned her head to look
  Towards the darkening beach:
Neighbours here and neighbours there
  Heard one scream, as if a bird
Shrilly screaming cleft the air:–
  That was all they heard.

Jessie she comes home no more,
  Comes home never;
Her lover's step sounds at his door
  No more forever.
And boats may search upon the sea
  And search along the river,
But none know where the bodies be:
  Sea-winds that shiver,
Sea-birds that breast the blast,
  Sea-waves swelling,
Keep the secret first and last
  Of their dwelling.

Whether the tide so hemmed them round
  With its pitiless flow,
That when they would have gone they found
  No way to go;
Whether she scorned him to the last
  With words flung to and fro,
Or clung to him when hope was past,
  None will ever know:
Whether he helped or hindered her,
  Threw up his life or lost it well,
The troubled sea, for all its stir
  Finds no voice to tell.

Only watchers by the dying
  Have thought they heard one pray
Wordless, urgent; and replying
  One seem to say him nay:
And watchers by the dead have heard
  A windy swell from miles away,
With sobs and screams, but not a word
  Distinct for them to say:
And watchers out at sea have caught
  Glimpse of a pale gleam here or there,
Come and gone as quick as thought,
  Which might be hand or hair.

- churl – peasant
- bane – destruction/ruin
- unked – alien/stange
- strand – beach

QUESTIONS

1. The verse form is a stanza made up of three ballad-form
   stanzas, and mainly following the rhythm and rhyme of
   ballad form. Describe ballad form, and identify places

where Rossetti deviates from this form, either in rhythm or rhyme scheme.

2. How does the ballad rhythm suit the style of the story?

3. Explain how the sea is personified.

4. In your own words, describe Jessie Cameron's character. What are her good pints and bad points? What negative quality is described in stanza 4 and why is it partly responsible for her fate?

5. How is her character different from the expectation of a woman's character in 19th century England?

6. In your own words, describe the neighbour's son's character. What is unusual and strange about him? How do we know that he is truly devoted to Jessie?

7. Read the last five stanzas and describe in detail what happened to the two young people.

8. What language is used to give a heightened sense of tragedy?

9. How is sibilance (use of 's' sounds) alliteration and internal rhyme used throughout the poem?

10. The poem is written from the perspective of an omniscient narrator. However, this viewpoint shifts in stanza seven to that of her mother and neighbours. In your opinion, does this change of viewpoint work, or does it leave the reader unsatisfied?

COMMENTARY

The verse form which Rossetti uses is closely related to ballad form. Ballad form varies, but the commonest form is a four line stanza with alternating tetrameter and trimeter and a rhyme scheme of a b c b. Rossetti has combined three such stanzas and rhymed them more tightly, a b a b. She has also varied the line length on occasions: in stanza one, line three, an expected trimeter becomes a tetrameter, and in the last line of stanza four, an expected trimeter becomes a dimeter. This flexibility can also be found in traditional ballads. This ballad-like form is well-suited to her subject matter, and style of narration, which also resemble traditional ballads. However, her language and character descriptions are much more complex than those found in traditional ballads.

This is immediately apparent when we come to the personification of the sea, "the moaning sea", in stanza one. This is repeated later the poem, and is a foreshadowing of the tragedy that will take place.

The poem immediately plunges the reader into the middle of a heated argument, giving it great dramatic force and directness. The point of view character is Jessie Cameron, and her personality is described in detail in stanza two. Unlike the characters in traditional ballads, she is complex, with a mix of good and bad qualities. Above all, she is strong, proud and independent – very different from the refined, religious, subservient and modest ideal of Victorian womanhood. It is interest to compare and contrast Jessie's character to that of the author. It seems that Rossetti, though somewhat shy and retiring, also had a proud, independent character, and like Jessie, rejected her suitor (three of them, in fact). A key word in this description is 'free'. Most Victorian women were not free,

71

as there was little work for them to do and they relied on marriage to give them status.

Stanza three is puzzling, because Jessie's statement that he is "good for Madge, or good for Cis, Or good for Kate, may be" suggests that he is a very ordinary sort of man, whereas his description in stanza five suggests that he is anything but. It is interesting to compare this with a similar passage in *No, Thank You, John* where Rossetti writes: "I dare say Meg or Moll would take/ Pity upon you, if you'd ask." William Rossetti stated that this poem probably referred to her third suitor, John Brett. Could it be that this poem also contains reflections on her relationship with Brett? Perhaps the argument of the lovers echoes arguments that she had with Brett.

In the next stanza, Jessie's worst quality – pride – is emphasized through repetition. This is not the pride of a woman who admires herself in a mirror; it is not her appearance she is proud of, but of her dignity, independence and freedom. Christina Rossetti was a devout Christian and would have been well aware that pride was considered to be the most serious of the seven deadly sins and the source of all the others. The last two lines are important: "And in her foot, which might have fled, But would not fly." In other words, her pride is the cause of the disaster which overtakes her; she is tapping her foot with anger instead of running away from the incoming tide.

The fifth stanza describes the 'neighbour's son' who is trying to woo Jessie. The description is strange, and based on rumour. "some say". But there is an import qualification in the description: "Yet he had gone through fire and flood/ Only to win her smile." Thus, whatever the truth about him, he really loves her, despite rumours of "guile" (deceit). One of the strange things about this poem is that

72

an unusual suitor with the independence and free spirit implied by the phrase "gypsy blood" might have been attractive to a free-spirited woman like Jennie – and who knows, had the tide not come in, they might have come to an understanding. Perhaps there is an echo here of Rossetti's own life, where she rejected three lovers who seemed well suited to her: James Collinson, one of the PRB, and like her, a deeply religious man; Charles Cayley, with whom she retained a lifelong friendship; and John Brett, also an artist. Instead, like Jessie Cameron, she chose to remain "free".

In stanza six the focus shifts briefly to her mother putting a light out to guide her daughter home. The seventh stanza begins with a hint of the young peoples' new closeness, brought about by their shared danger. The focus shifts back to her mother again, and from that point all we ever hear about Jessie are guesses and ghostly rumours. Their tragedy is brought home by words such as: "shiver", "blast", "hemmed", and "pitiless", the latter word once again personifying the sea.

The penultimate stanza speculates about how the young people responded to each other in their peril, but the last stanza suggests that she continued to say "nay". It is interesting that this word reminds us of the rejection of a lover in the poem *Love From The North*.

Overall, the tone of the poem is gloomy and tragic. Two young people have an argument that distracts them and leads to their death, but even in the face of death, Jessie cannot surrender her pride.

In The Round Tower At Jhansi, June 8, 1857

A hundred, a thousand to one; even so;
Not a hope in the world remained:
The swarming, howling wretches below
Gained and gained and gained.

Skene looked at his pale young wife:–
"Is the time come?" – "The time is come!" –
Young, strong, and so full of life:
The agony struck them dumb.

Close his arm about her now,
Close her cheek to his,
Close the pistol to her brow–
God forgive them this!

"Will it hurt much?" – "No, mine own:
I wish I could bear the pang for both."
"I wish I could bear the pang alone:
Courage, dear, I am not loth."

Kiss and kiss: "It is not pain
Thus to kiss and die.
One kiss more." – "And yet one again." –
"Good by." – "Good by."

• loth – reluctant

BACKGROUND

The incident described in this poem took place during
the Indian Mutiny of 1857 to 1859. The rebellion began as a

74

mutiny of sepoys of the East India Company's army on 10 May 1857, partly because they had to bite open rifle cartridges which were greased with tallow derived from beef and pork which was again the religion of both Hindus and Muslims. Jhansi became the centre of the rebellion. A small group of Company officials and their families took refuge in Jhansi Fort, and the Rani (princess) negotiated their evacuation. However, when they left the fort they were massacred by the rebels over whom the Rani had no control. The Europeans suspected the Rani of complicity, despite her repeated denials.

This is how the National Army Museum describes the incident:

Mrs Skene and her husband, Captain Alexander Skene of the 68th Bengal Native Infantry, were killed at Jhansi Fort on 8 June 1857 during the Indian Mutiny (1857-1859). Captain Skene was British superintendent at Jhansi. At the first sign of unrest, he had ordered all Christians in Jhansi to take refuge in the fort. They remained under siege there until 8 June when the rebels offered to spare their lives if they surrendered the fort. Skene agreed, believing that the Rani of Jhansi had guaranteed their safety, but the 56 Christians were all hacked to death with swords. The Rani's personal responsibility for the massacre is still hotly debated.

Rossetti appended a footnote to her poem in 1875: "I retain this little poem, not as historically accurate, but as written and published before I heard the supposed facts of its first verse contradicted." She had come across an account of the incident that stated that the Skene family had been captured and killed and had not committed suicide. However, what actually happened has never been discovered, and the version of events described in her poem may well be the true one.

QUESTIONS

1. How does Rossetti's account differ from the account given by the National Army Museum?

2. Why might people in this situation choose to commit suicide?

3. Explain how the verse form contributes to the sense of panic in the poem. (Hint: look particularly how anapaests are used). Read the lines aloud and consider the effect of the rhythm.

4. In your opinion, would the poem have been better if it had been much longer and contained more description?

5. How is the hopelessness of the situation emphasized in the first stanza? Why is it important to establish that the situation is totally hopeless?

6. What is the effect of the three words used to describe the rebels?

7. How is repetition used for emphasis throughout the poem?

8. Look at the use of anaphora in stanza three, what change of emphasis happens in the third line and what is its effect?

9. What is the significance of the line: "God forgive them this!" Comment on the use of the word "them" rather than "us" in terms of narrative perspective. In whose voice is this line?

10. Stanza four consists of terse dialogue without reporting

clauses (e.g., "she said"). Describe the emotions that each speech reveals.

11. What is the effect of the repeated word "kiss" in the last stanza?

12. What emotions are you left with after reading the poem?

13. Suggest three words that describe the tone of the poem.

COMMENTARY

The poem begins "in media res", a Latin term for "in the middle of the action". This was possible because readers at the time would have known about the Indian Mutiny, and many would have heard of this particular incident. Beginning in this way adds drama and excitement, and is also one of the components of the poem's powerful simplicity.

The verse form is also simple: a four line stanza with alternate tetrameters and trimeters rhymed a b a b. A sense of urgency and panic is imparted by frequent use of anapaestic feet, as can be seen in this analysis:

Anapaest   Anapaest   Iamb
X X /   X X   /   X   /
not a hope in the world remained

Note the connotations of the words to describe the rebels: "swarming" has connotations of a plague of insects, "howling" is a noise associated with a pack of wolves, and "wretch" is synonymous with words like: scoundrel, villain, ruffian, rogue, rascal, reprobate, criminal. In *Frankenstein*, Mary Shelley refers to the monster as a "wretch". Thus the rebels are presented as being very far from honourable soldiers, and more like animals or the worse types of humans.

The question in stanza two raises the suspense: "Is the time come?" – for what? we wonder. The situation suggests something terrible. The next two lines form a strong contrast which have a tragically ironic force. They are "Young, strong..." but they face certain death.

The next stanza makes powerful use of anaphora. The first two lines emphasise the closeness of man and wife, but the third, using the same grammatical structure, completely changes the focus. It is a pistol – the means of death – which is close now. The final line is an interpolation by the author. Rossetti, a deeply Christian woman, is horrified by the thought, that, in the words of Hamlet, that God has "fixed/His canon 'gainst self slaughter". However, she understands the extremity of their situation. If they are captured, Captian Skene would be tortured, and his wife suffer what often called in literature "a fate worse than death".

The conversation in stanza four is terse, emphasising their haste, as little time is left before they are overwhelmed. The terseness and pace is created by the lack of reporting clauses or description of their emotions. Yet their emotions are clear enough: love and self-sacrifice, both would die for the other. In the last line the wife reassures her husband about what he has to do.

Their poignancy of their parting in the final stanza is emphasized by repetition, particularly of the word "kiss" and also of the "good by". The tragedy is further emphasized by the juxtaposition of the word "kiss" and "die".

The tone of the poem is courageous, tragic, moving, loving, self-sacrificing. The nobility in suicide of the two married people contrasts with the barbarism of the attackers.

Remember

Remember me when I am gone away,
Gone far away into the silent land;
When you can no more hold me by the hand,
Nor I half turn to go yet turning stay.
Remember me when no more day by day
You tell me of our future that you planned:
Only remember me; you understand
It will be late to counsel then or pray.
Yet if you should forget me for a while
And afterwards remember, do not grieve:
For if the darkness and corruption leave
A vestige of the thoughts that once I had,
Better by far you should forget and smile
Than that you should remember and be sad.

QUESTIONS

1. What is the name of the verse form of this poem?

2. If the name of the verse for is x, what kind of x is it?

3. What is the rhyme scheme? Where is the division between the first part and the second part? What is the literary term for these parts?

4. What is the rhyme scheme and stanza-structure of the earlier kind of verse form x used in England? Who is the most popular writer of this kind of verse form x?

5. What is the message that the speaker in the poem wishes to convey to her lover?

6. What is the "silent land"? If it is death, or the afterlife, how does it differ from the Christian concept of the afterlife?

7. What other words in the poem describe death? Are they positive or negative? What do they make you think of?

8. How is the word "remember" used throughout the poem. What does it refer on the different occasions it is used?

9. Is there anything contradictory in the way she juxtaposes the word "remember" with the word "forget"?

10. Explain the paradox in the last two lines.

11. Compare and contrast the poem with *Song: When I Am Dead, My Dearest*.

12. Compare with Shakespeare's Sonnet 71, *No Longer Mourn for Me When I Am Dead*.

COMMENTARY

In 1849 Rossetti had a serious illness. At this time she was engaged to James Collinson, so it is likely that she had him in mind when she wrote it.

The poem is a Petrarchan sonnet. This kind of sonnet is characterized by being divided into an octet and sestet. Even though the lines are often printed in one block, there is usually a shift of emphasis from the octet to the sestet, and that is the case in this poem, where the shift is marked by the word "yet". The form differs from the Elizabethan (often known as the Shakespearean) sonnet which has three stanzas rhymed a b a b and ends with a couplet (though, again, they lines are often printed as one block). This arrangement gives an epigrammatic force to the end of the sonnet.

The poem begins with an exhortation to a loved one to remember the narrator (whether author or persona) when she is gone into the "silent land". This we take as a metaphor for death and what is beyond it. If we put this together with the words "darkness and corruption" which we find later in the poem, we may be forgiven for wondering what has happened to Rossetti's Christianity (which is sometimes described as "fanatical"). This is not the Christian heaven (where, according to the Bible, Cherubim and Seraphim praise God continually). Further, a Christian believes that "darkness and corruption" is followed by resurrection. Is this evidence of doubt in Rossetti?

She celebrates the things that they, as lovers can do in life: "hold me by the hand", "yet turning stay", "our future that you planned", though some critics have seen a discordant note here. Why "you" and not "we"? Could her detached attitude to being remembered result from reservations about the relationship? Probably not. It is more likely to be a standard Victorian female attitude that slips by the usually independent minded Rossetti.

The seset brings us to the point of the poem which is the irony that she prefers her lover to forget her and be happy, than remember her and be sad. What she is saying is that she loves him so much (this might be the meaning of "the thoughts that I once had", but why "thoughts" and not "feelings"?) that she wants him to be happy even if it means forgetting her.

It is interesting to compare this poem to *Song: When I Am Dead, My Dearest*. It is essentially a more sophisticated treatment of the same idea, though the speaker in *Song: When I Am Dead, My Dearest* is much more detached and indifferent.

Somewhere or Other

Somewhere or other there must surely be
The face not seen, the voice not heard,
The heart that not yet– never yet– ah me!
Made answer to my word.

Somewhere or other, may be near or far;
Past land and sea, clean out of sight;
Beyond the wandering moon, beyond the star
That tracks her night by night.

Somewhere or other, may be far or near;
With just a wall, a hedge, between;
With just the last leaves of the dying year
Fallen on a turf grown green.

QUESTIONS

1. Describe the verse form of the poem.

2. What is the narrator of this poem looking for?

3. How might we relate this poem to Rossetti's life?

4. What can you deduce from lines three and four of the first stanza? What is the effect of "ah me!"?

5. In stanza two, how does Rossetti use poetic language to express the idea that the longed for person (perhaps we can risk a cliché and call him a "soulmate") may be very far away.

6. How does she express the idea in stanza three that he might be very near?

7. What is the irony in the third stanza?

8. Where is the hint of sadness in the last stanza? What does this suggest about her chance of meeting that (to use another cliché) "special person".

COMMENTARY

Rossetti uses a simple, but unusual verse form, a four line stanza consisting of a pentameter, a tetrameter, a pentameter and a trimeter, rhymed a b a b. Each stanza begins in the same way, like a kind of refrain, emphasizing the speaker's desperate cry. The simple form is appropriate to the simplicity of the subject, though sophistication and depth is added by the hint of melancholy in the last stanza.

In the first stanza, the speaker, perhaps Rossetti herself, expresses the hope – and we know it is a desperate hope because of the word "surely" which suggest that she has been waiting for a long time, but been disappointed. Lines three and four make it clear that what she is looking for is a lover who is in totally sympathy with her – a 'soulmate' to use a modern expression. The desire for mutual sympathy and understanding is expressed in the line "made answer to my word", and the despair that she has not yet found such a person is expressed in line three, particularly in the interjection "ah me!"

We can relate this to Rossetti's life, because, though she had three suitors she rejected them, perhaps because she was searching for some impossible ideal; an impossible dream of perfect romantic love (though other poems

85

suggest it was because she valued her independence and freedom).

The second stanza expresses the idea that such a person may be very far away in hyperbolic terms: "Beyond the wandering moon, beyond the star". (She is not, of course referring to some alien lover with green skin and eight tentacles, just emphasing the idea of great distance).

This is leading into the last stanza where she emphasizes how close he might be: "With just a wall, a hedge, between". There is great irony in the fact that "the face not seen, the voice not heard" even though he is so close by. The poems ends with a note of sadness in "the last leaves of the dying year" suggesting that time is passing, her life is running out, and she still has not met that "special person". There is an almost haiku-like quality in the stanza, as the references to nature is like the kigo in Japanese poetry, a word or phrase associated with a particular season that creates a mood.

The tone of the poem is pleading, desperate, despairing and melancholy. The speaker seems to have little hope that she will find her soulmate.

The P.R.B.

The P.R.B. is in its decadence:–
for Woolner in Australia cooks his chops;
And Hunt is yearning for the land of Cheops;
D. G. Rossetti shuns the vulgar optic;
While William M. Rossetti merely lops
His B.s in English disesteemed as Coptic;
Calm Stephens in the twilight smokes his pipe
But long the dawning of his public day;
And he at last, the champion, great Millais
Attaining academic opulence
Winds up his signature with A.R.A.:–
So rivers merge in the perpetual sea,
So luscious fruit must fall when over ripe,
And so the consummated P.R.B.

- Land of Cheops - Egypt
- Coptic – a language descended from ancient Egyptian
- ARA – post-nominals which mean: Associate of the Royal Academy

It's not very enlightening to read a poem about people and events you know nothing about. But have a go, anyway. Read the poem and discuss what you make of it before you read the background notes.

BACKGROUND

The P.R.B. was written by Christina Rossetti in November 1853 following the breaking up of the Pre-Raphaelite Brotherhood throughout that year. In 1848,

Rossetti's brothers, Dante Gabriel and William Michael, along with James Collinson, John Everett Millais, Frederic George Stephens, Thomas Woolner and William Holman Hunt, founded the Pre-Raphaelite Brotherhood. They sought to model their work on the style of art and poetry that was popular before the time of the Italian High Renaissance painter Raphael (1483-1520), because they believed that the style of painting that succeeded him was too artificial and formulaic. It was William Michael Rossetti who recorded the aims of the Pre-Raphaelite Brotherhood at their founding meeting in September 1848:

> To have genuine ideas to express;
> To study nature attentively, so as to know how to express them;
> To sympathize with what is direct and serious and heartfelt in previous art, to the exclusion of what is conventional and self-parading and learned by rote;
> And most indispensable of all, to produce thoroughly good pictures and statues.

Below is some brief information about the names in the poem:

Thomas Woolner RA (1825 –1892) was the only sculptor among the original members. After participating in the foundation of the PRB, Woolner emigrated to Australia.

William Holman Hunt OM (1827 – 1910) was one of the outstanding painters of the PRB. His paintings were notable for their great attention to detail, vivid color, and elaborate symbolism. Hunt left England for Egypt in January 1854, spending two years in Egypt ("Land of Cheops") and the Holy Land.

Dante Gabriel Rossetti (1828 – 1882) was a poet,

illustrator, painter and translator. He was later to be the main inspiration for a second generation of artists and writers influenced by the movement, most notably William Morris and Edward Burne-Jones. His work also influenced the European Symbolists and was a major precursor of the Aesthetic movement. Perhaps the phrase "shuns the vulgar optic" in the poem refers to the fact that his paintings were more stylized than realistic.

William Michael Rossetti (1829 –1919) was a writer and critic. He was the brother of Maria Francesca Rossetti, Dante Gabriel Rossetti and Christina Georgina Rossetti. He became the movement's unofficial organizer and bibliographer. He worked full-time as a civil servant, but maintained a prolific output of criticism and biography across a range of interests. Perhaps Rossetti's comment in the poem refers to the fact that he was spending a lot of time writing about other things than the PRB.

Frederic George Stephens (1827 – 1907) was an art critic, and one of the two 'non-artistic' members of the Pre-Raphaelite Brotherhood.

Sir John Everett Millais, 1st Baronet, PRA (1829 –1896) had such prodigious artistic talent that he won a place at the Royal Academy schools at the unprecedented age of eleven. The Royal Academy valued exactly those principles that the PRB wished to rebel against. Later in life, he became President of the Royal Academy.

QUESTIONS

1. Look up the meaning of the word "decadence" and discuss its connotations. What evidence of decadence can be seen in the criticisms in the poem.

2. Describe the verse form of the poem. What is the rhyme scheme?

3. Make a list of the criticism of each person in the poem. Use the background notes to help you understand them.

4. After the list of criticisms expressed in humorous terms, Rossetti sums up as follows:

> So rivers merge in the perpetual sea,
> So luscious fruit must fall when over ripe,
> And so the consummated P.R.B.

What do you think she means by the first and second of these lines?

5. What does she mean by "consummated"? Look up the word and explore its connotations before attempting to answer the question.

6. Rossetti herself jokingly referred to this poem as "doggerel". Look up this word and say whether you agree.

7. What is Rossetti's attitude to the "decadence" of the PRB? Is it critical, mocking, regretful or accepting?

COMMENTARY

The poem is a gentle satire on the break up of the PRB. The word "decadence" which she uses in the first line means: "The act or process of falling into an inferior condition or state; deterioration; decay; decline; degeneration." Rossetti then goes on to explain why, giving a humorous critique of each of the members of the brother hood. We can see as soon as we read the second line that her approach will be humorous ridicule, "cooks his chops" being a slang way of saying "gets a suntan". So instead of creating a new kind of sculpture, Woolner is sunbathing (or perhaps the phrase means, "cooks his food"). They rhyme at the end of the next line is also humorous. "Land of Cheops" is a round about way of saying Egypt (the Great Pyramid is also known as the Pyramid of Cheops). As it happens both artists returned to do some of their best work, but, of course, Rossetti did not know this at the time. The comment about William Rossetti is unclear, but it seems to be a way of saying that his writing is not good (because it is as "disesteemed" as Coptic, a little-known language descended from Ancient Egyptian). Again, this is clearly intended as a joke. Stephens is relaxing, smoking a pipe, instead of doing serious creative work. She then moves on to Millais, whom she describes as the "champion" of the group, as he was arguably the best painter of the PRB. Her criticism of him is that he proudly uses his ARA (Associate of the Royal Academy) post-nominals, even though the PRB were sworn to a different set of artistic values. The suggestion is that these values were adversely affecting his painting.

The last three lines give her conclusion in two powerful images. "Rivers merge in the perpetual sea" seems to suggest that the uniqueness of the PRB style will inevitably be influenced by others and eventually become indistinguishable from them. The second image is the falling of over ripe fruit. The word "luscious" is a tribute to the achievements of the PRB – the word describes well their paintings full of vivid colour and rich imagery, but the phrase "over ripe" suggest that they have passed the peak of their achievement. She ends by describing the PRB as "consummated". "Consummation" means the ultimate end.

However, members of the original PRB went on to do

some of their best work, for example, Thomas Woolner, returned from Australia a year later and created many fine sculptures, his largest commission being the architectural sculptures for the Manchester Assize Courts. Holman Hunt did some of his best work in the Middle East, for example *The Scapegoat*, *The Finding of the Saviour in the Temple* and *The Shadow of Death*. There was also a second wave of artists influence by the PRB (see above).

In An Artist's Studio

One face looks out from all his canvasses,
One selfsame figure sits or walks or leans;
We found her hidden just behind those screens,
That mirror gave back all her loveliness.
A queen in opal or in ruby dress,
A nameless girl in freshest summer greens,
A saint, an angel; – every canvass means
The same; one meaning, neither more nor less.
He feeds upon her face by day and night,
And she with true kind eyes looks back on him
Fair as the moon and joyful as the light:
Not wan with waiting, not with sorrow dim;
Not as she is, but was when hope shone bright;
Not as she is, but as she fills his dream.

BACKGROUND

The "one face" referred to in the first line is Elizabeth
Siddal (1829 – 1862). This is confirmed by William
Michael's statement that the poem was about Dante
Gabriel's studio and his portraits of Siddal. Dante Gabriel
Rossetti met her in 1849, and by 1851, he began to paint
her to the exclusion of almost all other models. The
number of paintings he did of her number in the thousands.
Her health began to decline in 1852, probably due to
tuberculosis, but perhaps due to an intestinal disorder,
anorexia or addiction to laudanum. She died in 1862. Later
Rossetti used many different models, but all have a similar
look in his paintings, which is a stylized version of
Elizabeth Siddal, with whom he was still obsessed.

QUESTIONS

1. What is the name of the verse form of this poem? For more questions about this form, see the questions on *Remember*.

2. What is referred to by "those screens" and "that mirror"? (are they real or metaphorical screens and mirror?)

3. List the different guises in which Elizabeth Siddal appears (include different poses, roles and settings).

4. How would you interpret "every canvass means the same" (think about what Rossetti feels for Elizabeth)? Explain how this can be, given the different poses, roles and settings.

5. Which line in the poem shows that Dante Gabriel loves Siddal to the point of obsession? Explain the metaphor that gives force to the line.

6. Which line shows her feelings for him? Do they suggest that her feelings are equally intense?

7. The last four lines contain an important contrast between how Dante Gabriel sees her, and how she really is. See the note on her health, above. In your own words, describe how she is, and describe how he sees her. What are the key words that give power to these descriptions?

8. Comment on the use of anaphora in the poem.

9. Suggest some words to describe the tone of the poem.

COMMENTARY

The poem is a Petrarchan sonnet. The studio of the title is Dante Gabriel Rossetti's, the "one face" is Elizabeth Siddal, Dante Gabriel's model and lover (see background notes). The poet begins by commenting on the similarity underlying all the different poses, roles and settings of the paintings she has modeled for. The "screens" and the "mirror" are metaphors for Dante Gabriel's canvases. The octet builds up to the significant statement "every canvass means the same" – in other words, it means that he loves her.

The first line of the sestet shows that his love is obsessive by use of the metaphor "feeds upon her face". Food is an essential of life; in other words, Dante Gabriel cannot live without her. We might also see vampirish or cannibalistic connotations in these lines, all of which emphasise that Dante Gabriel's love is obsessive. The next line, as contrast, show that she loves him in return, but in a more reasonable and less intense manner. The key words being "kind" and "true". Let us not underestimate the value of these qualities. Shakespeare himself wrote : "fair, kind and true is all my argument". He was writing about a "fair youth", a young man, but, hey, love is love! Elizabeth Siddal has all these qualities. "Fair" (beautiful) appears in the next line in a beautiful simile comparing her to the moon, and her personal quality of joyousness is compared to the light.

So far, so good, but the poem has a disturbing ending. In the next line, "wan" (pale) is contrasted with "fair as the moon" and "dim" with "light". The two other significant words are "waiting" which probably refers to her incurable illness – she was waiting for death; and "sorrow" – because of her illness. Yet in the last lines we see that Dante Gabriel, because of his obsession, still sees her as she was when "hope shone bright" (another word in the lexical field of light), and anaphora is used to emphasise that he does not see her as she is but as he thinks she is – as she "fills his dream". The tone of the poem changes from pleasantly descriptive, celebrating variety, beauty and love, in the octet, to disturbing and dark in the sestet.

No, Thank You, John

I never said I loved you, John:
Why will you tease me day by day,
And wax a weariness to think upon
With always "do" and "pray"?

You know I never loved you, John;
No fault of mine made me your toast:
Why will you haunt me with a face as wan
As shows an hour-old ghost?

I dare say Meg or Moll would take
Pity upon you, if you'd ask:
And pray don't remain single for my sake
Who can't perform the task.

I have no heart? – Perhaps I have not;
But then you're mad to take offence
That don't give you what I have not got:
Use your common sense.

Let bygones be bygones:
Don't call me false, who owed not to be true:
I'd rather answer "No" to fifty Johns
Than answer "Yes" to you.

Let's mar our pleasant days no more,
Song-birds of passage, days of youth:
Catch at today, forget the days before:
I'll wink at your untruth.

Let us strike hands as hearty friends;
No more, no less; and friendship's good:

Only don't keep in view ulterior ends,
And points not understood

In open treaty. Rise above
Quibbles and shuffling off and on:
Here's friendship for you if you like; but love,-
No, Thank You, John.

- wax – grow
- tease – here, "pester"
- pray – please
- toast – not heated bread! This word can also mean: one that is highly admired
- mar – spoil
- bird of passage – a person who passes through a place without staying for long.

BACKGROUND

It is almost certain that this poem is autobiographical and refers to her relationship with the artist, John Brett. Rossetti probably felt comfortable about keeping the name "John" because the name is often used to refer to a 'generic' lover (look up "Dear John letter" on the Internet, and see the folk song *O No, John! No*). There is also other compelling evidence. In *Family Letters of Christina Rossetti* (1908), William Michael Rossetti writes:

Yet John was not absolutely mythical for, in one of her volumes which I possess, Christina made a pencil jotting, "The original John was obnoxious because he never gave scope for No, Thank You". This John was, I am sure the marine painter John Brett who (at a date long antecedent, say 1852) had appeared to be somewhat smitten with Christina.

QUESTIONS

1. Describe the verse form.

2. Comment on the use of alliteration in the poem.

3. Reread Rossetti's biography and the background notes about and try to relate this poem to Rossetti's life.

4. This poem can be classified as a "dramatic monologue". Why? Justify the appropriateness of both of the words in the phrase "dramatic monologue".

5. Though a dramatic monologue, we can hear an echo in the speaker's words of what John said. Make a list of, or underline his words. If you have time, rewrite the poem in prose as a dialogue.

6. How does the speaker, probably Rossetti herself, feel about her lover? Pick out key words and phrases that reveal her feelings. What are her reasons for rejecting John?

7. What do we learn about how John has conducted his courtship and made his proposals? What kind of a suitor is he?

8. What is your opinion about the tone of this speech to John? Is Rossetti being too harsh, too cruel? What do we learn about John's behaviour towards Rossetti that might justify such a firm response?

9. In what sense can the poem be described as humorous?

10. Explain the simile in stanza two. What does it tell us about John?

11. Stanza six is hard to understand. Explain what is the speaker is saying in simple words. What does the metaphor "Song-birds of passage" refer to? What is the "untruth" he tells?

12. What "ulterior ends" (alternative motives) might John have in continuing their friendship?

13. Is it possible for a man and woman to be close friends?

14. Compare and contrast this poem with the well-known folk song *O No, John! No*. How likely is it that Rossetti had this song in mind when writing her poem?

O No, John! No

BOY
On yonder hill there stands a creature
Who she is I do not know;
I'll go ask her hand in marriage,
She must answer yes or no.

GIRL
O no, John! No, John! No, John! No!

My father was a Spanish captain,
Went to sea a month ago;
First he kissed me then he left me,
Bid me always answer no.

O no, John! No, John! No, John! No!

BOY
O Madam in your face is beauty,
On your lips red roses grow;
Will you take me for your husband?
Madam answer yes or no.

GIRL
O no, John! No, John! No, John! No!

BOY
O Madam I will give you jewels,
I will make you rich and free,
I will give you silken dresses;
Madam will you marry me?

GIRL
O no, John! No, John! No, John! No!

BOY
O Madam since you are so cruel,
And that you do scorn me so,
If I may not be your husband?
Madam will you let me go?

GIRL
O no, John! No, John! No, John! No!

BOY
Then I will stay with you forever,
If you will not be unkind;
Madam, I have vowed to love you;
Would you have me change my mind?

GIRL
O no, John! No, John! No, John! No!

BOY
O hark! I hear the church bells ringing,
Will you come and be my wife?
Or, dear Madam, have you settled
To live single all your life?

GIRL
O no, John! No, John! No, John! No!

COMMENTARY

In *No, Thank You, John*, which is almost certainly
autobiographical, the author firmly rejects her lover's latest
proposal of marriage. The verse from is a four line stanza
consisting of tetrameters rhymed a b a b. The style of the
poem is dramatic monologue. We never hear John directly,
but his words are echoed by the speaker to the extent that it

possible to imagine the dialogue. It is clear that he has proposed to her many times, pleaded with her, and tried many arguments to persuade her, for example, he must have said: "I'll remain single if you don't marry me"; "You have no heart!"; "You are false!"

The simile of the ghost in the second stanza shows how deeply John loves the speaker, but it is also clear from the first line that she has never encouraged his love: "I never said I loved you".

She tells him to find other women, though in a condescending way, because she doesn't say they would love him but that they would "take pity on him". This sentiment echoes the words of Jessie Cameron:

> You're good for Madge, or good for Cis,
> Or good for Kate, may be:
> But what's to me the good of this
> While you're not good for me?'

Could this poem also have drawn upon Rossetti's personal experiences of rejecting John Brett? "Meg" and "Moll" are common names (well, they were at the time). Common in the sense of being numerous, but also in the sense of being associated with ordinary working people. They are not "sophisticated" names such as Clarissa, Rebecca, or, indeed, Christina. Therefore, Rossetti seems ot be suggesting that an ordinary, uneducated girl might be appropriate for John, and by implication, that she finds him uninteresting as a person.

When he accused her of having no heart, she replies that she cannot give what she has not got, i.e., love for him, and urges him to use his "common sense". This is a serious put down, almost as though she is rebuking a child.

Stanza five is hard to interpret. It seems that John has been referring to times in the past when they were closer. She replies that, whatever he might have thought at the time, she did not promise anything, and emphasises the fact with hyperbole: "I'd rather answer "No" to fifty Johns/ Than answer 'Yes' to you."

Stanza six is even harder. She seems to be saying that all this talk of what happened in the past is spoiling the pleasantness of the present. In the past, they were "birds of passage" (people who passed through a place without staying for long). "Song-birds", perhaps, because some beautiful words were shared. She urges him to live in the present and forget that past. The line "I'll wink at your untruth" suggests that he used those memories to imply that she made a promise to him.

She ends by offering her friendship, provided that he accepts it without "ulterior ends". In other words, in the hope that she will change her mind. She ends with the firm message, which is the title of the poem, "No, Thank You, John".

Some critics have described the tone of the poem as humorous, but if it is, it is dark humour, as there are too many cutting remarks and put-downs. Poor John is treated with scant respect, and many other critics do not find this funny.

Feminist critics, who are keen to claim Rossetti for their cause, have seen feminist values in this poem. For example, Simon Avery, in *Christina Rossetti: Gender and Power*, writes:

"What this poem asserts is the woman's right to say 'no' and to claim independence and agency for herself. Certainly, she is not to be bullied into a relationship because a man or social convention more generally demands it."

However, if we compare this poem to the folk song *O No, John! No*, we can see that independent, strong-minded women are not just a product of the 19th century intellectual elite. The song is a traditional song from Somerset, which was already ancient when collected by Cecil Sharp in the late 19th century. The song is remarkable similar to Rossetti's poem, to the extent that she may be parodying it. The woman in the song is just as determined to turn down her suitor as the speaker in Rossetti's poem, though the suitor seems to have much better arguments than John Brett: he flatters her, he offers her riches and fine clothes, and promises to be true to her forever. His final argument is to put pressure on her by saying that he can hear the church bells ringing. At the end of the last verse, the refrain of the song is used with an ironic twist. Will she be single all her life? "O no, John! No, John! No, John! No!" In that sense, she has gone one better than Rossetti.

A Daughter of Eve

A fool I was to sleep at noon
And wake when night is chilly
Beneath the comfortless cold moon:
A fool to pluck my rose too soon,
A fool to snap my lily.

My garden-plot I have not kept;
Faded and all-forsaken,
I weep as I have never wept:
Oh it was summer when I slept,
It's winter now I waken.

Talk what you please of future spring,
And sun-warmed sweet to-morrow:-
Stripped bare of hope and everything,
No more to laugh, no more to sing,
I sit alone with sorrow.

NOTE

This poem is based on nature symbolism: *noon, night, moon, rose, lily, garden, summer, winter, spring, sun.* Unfortunately, symbols are slippery things as their meaning is created by the culture of a particular time and place. However, Rossetti uses the traditional associations of recent European culture, so interpretation should not be too difficult.

QUESTIONS

1. Play a word association game with a partner. Take it in turn to say words from the list in the Note, while your partner responds with their immediate associations.

2. Where appropriate, group the symbols into opposites.

3. What can we deduce from the title?

4. Analyse the verse form of the poem.

5. Comment on the use of alliteration in this poem.

6. Using what you have said about the symbols, and bearing in mind Rossetti's biography, try to interpret each stanza in turn.

7. In the third stanza she is responding to someone who seems to be trying to reassure her. How does the person attempt to do this and what is her reply?

8. Suggest some words to describe the tone of the poem.

9. The phrase "Daughter of Eve" is often used to refer to women in general. How much in the poem could be seen as the common experience of all women, and how much is unique to Rossetti's life?

10. Compare and contrast this poem with the folk song *Let No Man Steal Your Thyme*. See next page.

Let No Man Steal Your Thyme

Come all you fair and tender maids
That flourish in your prime.
Beware, beware keep your garden fair.
Let no man steal your thyme;
Let no man steal your thyme.

For when your thyme is past and gone,
He'll care no more for you,
And every place where your thyme was waste
Will all spread o'er with rue,
Will all spread o'er with rue.

For woman is a branchy tree,
And man's a clinging vine,
And from your branches carelessly
He'll take what he can find,
He'll take what he can find.

The gardener's son was standing by;
Three flowers he gave to me
The pink, the blue, and the violet, too,
And the red, red rosy tree,
The red, red, rosy tree.

But I forsook the red rose bush
and gained the willow tree,
So all the world might plainly see
How my love slighted me,
How my love slighted me.

COMMENTARY

A Daughter of Eve seems autobiographical. "Noon" possibly refers to the middle of Rossetti's life. She was "a fool to sleep", suggests that she regrets losing the opportunities she had for love; she was unaware what she was missing. "Night" is presumably age. "Cold moon" suggests lifelessness; she is too old and barren now to be loved. The two flower symbols are difficult to interpret. The rose is usually seen as a symbol of love and the lily of death, so the two symbols may simple reinforce the meaning of the previous three lines. But what does "pluck my rose" mean? Does it mean, give up on love? And what does, "snap my lily" mean? The lily can also symbolise chastity and virtue. Perhaps one of her relationships was sexual, and she later regretted it. However, this seems hard to believe of a fanatically Christian woman.

The "garden-plot" may be a symbol for her health and beauty which she has neglected over the years and is now "faded". "Garden" is used as a symbol in the same way in *Let No Man Steal Your Thyme* (see below). Summer and Winter are two opposite symbols referring to her youth and her old age (and paralleling "noon" and "night", and possibly "rose" and "lily" depending on how you interpret those symbols).

The last stanza is a reply to someone who is trying to console her. The use of nature imager continues as the person speaks of "a future spring", "spring" symbolising new growth. "Sun-warmed" suggests summer. But Rossetti can't help thinking that, unlike the seasons, there is no cyclical rejuvenation for humans (unless you believe in reincarnation). Therefore she is left with "sorrow" symbolised by the absence of laughter and singing.

The tone of the poem is strongly pessimistic. There is no mention here of the compensations of age (are there any?). She feels that she has wasted her youth and lost her chance for love and that all that is left for her is regret, coldness and sorrow – perhaps she should have given John another chance!

It is interesting to compare this poem with the traditional folk song, *Let No Man Steal Your Thyme*, in which a garden symbolises all the beauties and personal qualities of a young female, and thyme symbolises virginity. Other nature symbolism is used throughout the song. Rue is a plant, *Ruta graveolens*, which symbolises sorrow. Indeed, the word 'rue' also means sorrow. Thus, the advice to girls given in the song is that if you let a man steal your virginity you will feel sorrow. The nature imagery continues in verse three by comparing woman to a tree and man to a "clinging vine", which suggests the parasitical nature of the superficial affection offered by some men. The last lines emphasise that he'll take what he wants, and imply that he will then leave. The fourth and fifth verses rapidly tell the narrator's story through the language of flowers. He gave her "the red, red rosy tree" (rose = love), and as a result she gained the "willow tree". The willow, because of its slender, drooping branches in commonly seen as a symbol of sorrow and weeping. So we presume that he made her pregnant and left her. The song ends with a repeat of the first verse (which is the chorus, when sung) which is the girl's advice to other young girls.

The song is poignant rather than pessimistic. The beauty of the imagery compensating somewhat for the sadness of the story. It is arguable that the anonymous minstrel who composed that song, many centuries ago, did a better job of using nature symbolism that the 19th century poet.

Paradise: in a Dream

Once in a dream I saw the flowers
That bud and bloom in Paradise;
More fair they are than waking eyes
Have seen in all this world of ours.
And faint the perfume-bearing rose,
And faint the lily on its stem,
And faint the perfect violet
Compared with them.

I heard the songs of Paradise:
Each bird sat singing in his place;
A tender song so full of grace
It soared like incense to the skies.
Each bird sat singing to his mate
Soft cooing notes among the trees:
The nightingale herself were cold
To such as these.

I saw the fourfold River flow,
And deep it was, with golden sand;
It flowed between a mossy land
With murmured music grave and low.
It hath refreshment for all thirst,
For fainting spirits strength and rest:
Earth holds not such a draught as this
From east to west.

The Tree of Life stood budding there,
Abundant with its twelvefold fruits;
Eternal sap sustains its roots,
Its shadowing branches fill the air.
Its leaves are healing for the world,

Its fruit the hungry world can feed,
Sweeter than honey to the taste
And balm indeed.

I saw the gate called Beautiful;
And looked, but scarce could look, within;
I saw the golden streets begin,
And outskirts of the glassy pool.
Oh harps, oh crowns of plenteous stars,
Oh green palm-branches many-leaved—
Eye hath not seen, nor ear hath heard,
Nor heart conceived.

I hope to see these things again,
But not as once in dreams by night;
To see them with my very sight,
And touch, and handle, and attain:
To have all Heaven beneath my feet
For narrow way that once they trod;
To have my part with all the saints,
And with my God.

NOTES

As a devout, some would say fanatical, Christian, Rossetti knew her Bible very well, and makes many references to it in the poem.

"The fourfold River" is described in Genesis 2:10-14:

And a river went out of Eden to water the garden, and from thence it was parted, and became into four heads. And the name of the first is Pishon; that is it which encompasseth the whole land of Havilah, where there is gold; and the gold of that land is good; there is bdellium and the onyx stone. And the name of the second river is

Gihon; the same is it that encompasseth the whole land of Ethiopia. And the name of the third river is Riddekel; that is it which goeth toward the east of Assyria, and the fourth river is Euphrates.

"The Tree of Life" is described in Genesis 3:22-24:

And the LORD God said, Behold, the man is become as one of us, to know good and evil: and now, lest he put forth his hand, and take also of the tree of life, and eat, and live for ever.

The "twelvefold fruits" are described in Revelation 22:1-21:

Then the angel showed me the river of the water of life, bright as crystal, flowing from the throne of God and of the Lamb. Through the middle of the street of the city; also, on either side of the river, the tree of life with its twelve kinds of fruit, yielding its fruit each month. The leaves of the tree were for the healing of the nations.

"The gate called Beautiful" is decribed in Acts 3:1-5:

Now Peter and John went up together to the temple at the hour of prayer, the ninth hour. And a certain man lame from his mother's womb was carried, whom they laid daily at the gate of the temple which is called Beautiful, to ask alms from those who entered the temple; who, seeing Peter and John about to go into the temple, asked for alms.

Harps and palm leaves are described in many places, e.g., Revelation 14:2 (harps) and Revelation 7:9 (palm leaves).

QUESTIONS

1. Describe the verse form of the poem.

2. How is alliteration used in the poem?

3. In the first stanza, how does Rossetti emphasise the beauty of the flowers in Paradise?

4. Comment on the lines: "And faint the perfect violet/ Compared with them." If something is "perfect", how can something else of the same kind be better? Is this an error of logic or language on Rossetti's part, or a deliberate paradox?

5. Explain the simile: "soared like incense to the skies".

6. What other technique does she use to convey the beauty of the singing of the heavenly birds?

7. Pick out or underline words and phrases which describe the qualities of "the fourfold river".

8. What simile and what metaphor are used to describe the "Tree of Life".

9. What emotion does the repeated "oh" in stanza five convey?

10. How does the last stanza develop the idea expressed in the title that this glimpse of paradise is a dream?

11. How does the view of the afterlife expressed in this poem compare with that expressed in Remember?

12. If you dreamed of heaven, what would you see?

COMMENTARY

This poem was published in 1865, and is an early example of the religious poetry to which she devoted herself in later life.

The verse form consists mainly of tetrameters (with a final dimeter) and is rhymed a b b a c d e d.

She describes a vision of Paradise that she saw in a dream. She emphasises the incredible beauty of the flowers by saying that earthly flowers (and she mentions some of the most beautiful – the rose, the lily and violet) seem "faint" by comparison. Her use of the word "perfect" in line 7 is interesting, since the word is an absolute (nothing can be better than perfect). This is not a linguistic or logical mistake. It simply emphasises that what seems perfect to us is nothing when compared to the beauty of heavenly flowers. It is a powerful way of disconnecting our ideas of beauty from the mortal world and helping us to see that there is something far better in Paradise.

In stanza two Rossetti describes the birds which sing the "songs of Paradise". The comparison with incense is interesting. Incense floats upward to heaven like the birds' song. The reference shows Rossetti's High Church affiliation. The comparison with the nightingale is interesting. It is the same kind of comparison that she used in stanza one. The nightingale's song, considered to be one of the most beautiful, is "cold" compared to the song of the heavenly birds. Here Rossetti draws on the positive connotations of the nightingale's song, whereas in *When I Am Dead, My Dearest*, the connotations are negative.

The next three stanzas draw on descriptions of Paradise given in different books of the Bible which are explained in the Notes. Thus her vision is not freely imaginative; it is not a personal interpretation of Paradise, but one firmly based in scripture, as we would expect from a devout Christian. There is the "fourfold River" from Genesis, the "Tree of Life" from Revelations, and the "gate called Beautiful" from Acts. The refreshing qualities of the "fourfold River" are better than anything on earth, and the "twelvefold fruits" of the "Tree of Life" are praised with the conventional simile "sweeter than honey".

Streets of gold, a "glassy" pool (the adjective emphasising its clarity), harps, stars and palm-branches appear in stanza five, along with three "ohs" that indicate the ecstatic delight of the dreamer. The stanza ends with a repetition of the idea that such wonderful things have never been seen, or even conceived of, on earth.

The poem ends with a change of focus. Rossetti is no longer describing her dream, but speaking of her hope that she will see all these things for real. The reality of the experience being emphasised in the line: "And touch, and handle, and attain". Is there an unconscious echo of John's Gospel here, where the disciple Thomas (Doubting Thomas) says: "Unless I see the nail marks in his hands and put my finger where the nails were, and put my hand into his side, I will not believe." (John 20:24-29). Could it be that, deep down, she doubts that such a Paradise exists unless she can experience it physically? There are certainly doubts (or hints of doubts) in several of her poems.

The dimeter which ends the poem is powerful in its epigrammatic terseness: "And with my God", for this is what Paradise really is.

Paradise: in a Symbol

Golden-winged, silver-winged,
Winged with flashing flame,
Such a flight of birds I saw,
Birds without a name:
Singing songs in their own tongue
(Song of songs) they came.

One to another calling,
Each answering each,
One to another calling
In their proper speech:
High above my head they wheeled,
Far out of reach.

On wings of flame they went and came
With a cadenced clang,
Their silver wings tinkled,
Their golden wings rang,
The wind it whistled through their wings
Where in Heaven they sang.

They flashed and they darted
Awhile before mine eyes,
Mounting, mounting, mounting still
In haste to scale the skies—
Birds without a nest on earth,
Birds of Paradise.

Where the moon riseth not,
Nor sun seeks the west,
There to sing their glory
Which they sing at rest,
There to sing their love-song

When they sing their best:

Not in any garden
That mortal foot hath trod,
Not in any flowering tree
That springs from earthly sod,
But in the garden where they dwell,
The Paradise of God.

QUESTIONS

1. Give a definition of the term 'symbol'.

2. What is the evidence that these are not earthly birds?

3. What do the birds symbolise?

4. What song are the birds singing? What is the significance of this song?

5. Discuss the musical terms used to describe the sound of the birds' flight.

6. The birds are "far out of reach" for Rossetti. What symbolic meaning might this have?

7. Describe the verse form of the poem.

COMMENTARY

The title of the poem tells us that Rossetti sees these birds as symbolic. A symbol is something which stands for something else. Many symbols are conventional, such a rose symbolising love. Other symbols can be created by an author. For example, in *Shut Out*, Rossetti describes the garden in such a way that it symbolises Paradise. However, the birds in the poem are not earthly birds that have been described in a way that symbolises Paradise, they are actual "birds of Paradise" (though not to be confused with the *Paradisaeidae*, the species known as Bird-of-paradise). The first words of the poem make this clear with words such as "golden", "silver" and "flame". Later on, we learn that they make tinkling and ringing sounds, and that they "have no nests on earth".

They sing a beautiful song which Rossetti describes as the "Song of songs", almost certainly referring to *The Song of Songs*, also known as *The Song of Solomon*, in the Bible. This is a love song sung by two earthly lovers which is said to symbolise God's love for his people. Note that the description "love-song" is used in the penultimate stanza of Rossetti's poem.

Rossetti's comment in the second stanza that the birds are "out of reach" may be a hint of the religious doubt she expresses in some of her other poems (see *Shut Out*). Her doubt is, not that Paradise does not exist, but that she may not be worthy to get there. Nevertheless, the overall tone of the poem is joyous and celebratory. The birds symbolise the beauty of Paradise which all human beings have the opportunity to enter.

The verse form consists of six-line stanzas rhymed a b c b d b with alternating tetrameters and trimeters in a mainly trochaic rhythm. Note that stanza three is the most irregular, and whether the irregularity has some poetic effect, suggestive of the sounds described, or is merely awkward must be left to the judgment of the reader.

From the Antique

It's a weary life, it is, she said:
Doubly blank in a woman's lot:
I wish and I wish I were a man:
Or, better thcn any being, were not:

Were nothing at all in all the world,
Not a body and not a soul:
Not so much as a grain of dust
Or a drop of water from pole to pole.

Still the world would wag on the same,
Still the seasons go and come:
Blossoms bloom as in days of old,
Cherries ripen and wild bees hum.

None would miss me in all the world,
How much less would care or weep:
I should be nothing, while all the rest
Would wake and weary and fall asleep.

QUESTIONS

1. What are the implications of the seemingly unrelated title?

2. Describe the verse form of the poem.

3. Rosetti wishes for two things in this poem. What are they? Which does she long for the most and why?

4. The poem begins and ends with the word "weary".

Check the definition of this word. What are the things that make Rossetti feel this way (hint: look at the first and last stanzas)?

5. Re-read her biography and make a list of some of the things that might have made her feel "weary" of life.

6. Despite the negative tone of the poem, some positive things are mentioned (perhaps by accident). What are they?

7. In what sense does this poem express a feminist view of the world? Find out more about "a woman's lot" in Victorian Britain. What progress has been made since then?

8. Jot down a few words to describe the tone of the poem.

COMMENTARY

This is one of only a few poems in this selection that overtly discuss Rossetti's attitudes to gender issues (though the word "gender" was not used in that sense in those days). There are many more such poems in her complete works.

The title seems strangely unrelated to the poem, but perhaps suggests that the problems she describes, especially from a female perspective, have been going on since ancient times. It could also allude to the influence of one of her favourite poets, Sappho (c. 620-570 BC).

The first three lines lead us to believe that the poem is going to be about the inferior role "lot" of women in the 19th century Britain, but the focus shifts in the last line: if it is better to be a man than a woman, it is better to be nothing than anybody. It is this idea that is developed in the rest of the poem.

A full understanding of the poem depends on a full awareness of the connotations of the word "weary". The word means much more than merely physically tired. It also means "having one's patience, tolerance, or pleasure exhausted" – and that is how life makes Rossetti feel.

The second stanza emphasises the concept of nothingness in a way that a Buddhist might approve of. Each line pushes the idea of nothingness further with anaphora of "not of…"

The use of the slang expression "wag on" (not used today), is interesting as it conveys a word-weary cynicism. However, the rest of the stanza seems strangely positive. Blossoms, cherries and wild bees are things of beauty and never cause pain (unless the bees sting us!). It is arguable that this strikes a false note in the poem, and that it would have been better to have mentioned some of the negative things in nature, drought storm, etc.

The last stanza is more effective in conveying what makes her weary of life. She fears that nobody will miss her, or care or weep if she were not there. The poem was written in 1854 (four years after her "year of love"). Could this be the beginning of remorse for the lost chance of love that later became a common subject in her poems?

The stanza ends with a powerful line that effectively sums up the whole poem, repeating the word "weary" like the hint of a refrain: "all the rest/ Would wake and weary and fall asleep." The disappointment and exhaustion of life is cyclical and sleep itself is a kind of nothingness. Overall, the tone of the poem is pessimistic.

Echo

Come to me in the silence of the night;
Come in the speaking silence of a dream;
Come with soft rounded cheeks and eyes as bright
As sunlight on a stream;
Come back in tears,
O memory, hope, love of finished years.

O dream how sweet, too sweet, too bitter sweet,
Whose wakening should have been in Paradise,
Where souls brimfull of love abide and meet;
Where thirsting longing eyes
Watch the slow door
That opening, letting in, lets out no more.

Yet come to me in dreams, that I may live
My very life again though cold in death:
Come back to me in dreams, that I may give
Pulse for pulse, breath for breath:
Speak low, lean low
As long ago, my love, how long ago.

QUESTIONS

1. Comment on the significance of the title.

2. Describe the use of rhyme and alliteration in the poem.

3. How is anaphora and repetition used in the poem?

4. In stanza two, the poet speaks of "Paradise". Is this the
   Christian Heaven or the paradise of fulfilled love? Who

is she addressing in the poem? Christ or her lover? Give evidence for your answers.

5. Explain the figure of speech: "eyes as bright/ As sunlight on a stream".

6. In what sense can eyes be "thirsting" (stanza two, line four)?

7. These lines are difficult to interpret: "Watch the slow door/ That opening, letting in, lets out no more." What do you think they mean?

8. What words and phrases give sensuality to the last stanza?

9. Re-read Rossetti's biography and relate this poem to her life.

10. Suggest some words to describe the tone of the poem.

COMMENTARY

It is never easy to relate a poem to a poet's life, as the poet may be writing in the voice of a persona, or imitating a favourite poem by another poet. However, this poem seems part of a trend in Rossetti's poetry. It was written in 1854, and by then there is evidence to suggest that she was already regretting her lost chances of love. In this poem she expresses a yearning that her lover (I wonder which one) will come back to her in a dream. It can only be in a dream because the last line of the poem tells us that the intimacy they shared was "long ago".

As in many of her other poems, Rosetti makes extensive use of anaphora and repetition. "Come" is repeated four times, "sweet" three times. Two lines begin with the anaphora "where". It is interesting how the repetition of sweet includes the oxymoron "bitter sweet". This is probably one of the commonest oxymorons, but in this line it has a fresh power. The overall effect of all this repetition is to emphasise the sense of longing.

The word "Paradise" is interesting. The capitalisation of the word implies the Christian Paradise, Heaven. However, Rossetti is forgetting her theology here, because there are no male/female relationships in heaven. We are told this in several places in the Bible, for example: "For in the resurrection they neither marry, nor are given in marriage, but are as the angels of God in heaven" (Matthew 22:30). The door in line five is the door of Paradise (once you have been let in, you can't get out, and if it's as good as the Bible says, you wouldn't want to!) "Thirsting, longing eyes" is problematic. Souls in Paradise should be perfectly fulfilled and happy and thinking only of praising God. They should not be looking at the door of Paradise longing for their loved ones to arrive. What she is saying in this stanza is that, after dreaming of her love, she hopes to wake up in Paradise where she can watch the door for his arrival. Her feelings must have been very strong for her to muddle up her theology in this way!

The "yet" that begins the final stanza is the realisation that, for the time being, she can only meet her lover in dreams, and it is only in those dreams that she feels alive. Her real life is, by comparison, "cold as death". The poem ends with a moving evocation of their lost physical intimacy, which is very physical; they are aware of each others beating hearts, and their breathing. Their voices are "low" because they are so close, and the word "lean" describes how they press against each other. Overall the tone of the poem is yearning, melancholy, pessimistic.

Shut Out

The door was shut. I looked between
Its iron bars; and saw it lie,
My garden, mine, beneath the sky,
Pied with all flowers bedewed and green:

From bough to bough the song-birds crossed,
From flower to flower the moths and bees;
With all its nests and stately trees
It had been mine, and it was lost.

A shadowless spirit kept the gate,
Blank and unchanging like the grave.
I peering through said: 'Let me have
Some buds to cheer my outcast state.'

He answered not. 'Or give me, then,
But one small twig from shrub or tree;
And bid my home remember me
Until I come to it again.'

The spirit was silent; but he took
Mortar and stone to build a wall;
He left no loophole great or small
Through which my straining eyes might look:

So now I sit here quite alone
Blinded with tears; nor grieve for that,
For nought is left worth looking at
Since my delightful land is gone.

A violet bed is budding near,
Wherein a lark has made her nest:

And good they are, but not the best;
And dear they are, but not so dear.

QUESTIONS

1. Describe the verse form of the poem.

2. Comment on the use of alliteration in the poem.

3. The "garden" in this poem is almost certainly an allegory of Paradise, from which Rossetti feels shut out. Write the basic message of this poem in simple, non-allegorical language.

4. Which words in the first stanza emphasise the sense of exclusion?

5. Explain what the poet means when she writes: "It had been mine, and it was lost." (Hint: what entitles a Christian to Paradise, and what debars a Christian from Paradise?)

6. What are the beauties of the garden of Paradise?

7. What unusual adjective is used to describe the spirit? What simile is used to describe the spirit? Who or what do you think the spirit is?

8. In the next two stanzas, what does Rossetti ask for? What do these things represent? (Hard one, this, even if you're up on your theology! Have a guess.)

9. What does the spirit do, and how does it make her feel?

10. Re-read the last stanza and explain the lines: "And good they are, but not the best;/ And dear they are, but not so

dear." (Hint: she uses the same idea in her poem *Paradise: in a Dream*.)

11. Suggest some words to describe the tone of the poem.

12. Compare and contrast this poem with *Paradise: in a Dream*, and *Paradise: in a Symbol*.

COMMENTARY

Rossetti wrote devotional poetry all her life, and through it she expresses her beliefs, hopes and doubts. This poem expresses her doubt that she will be worthy of Paradise. It is an allegory in which Paradise is compared to a garden (a comparison she often uses), and she is shut out of that garden by a "shadowless spirit". The language of exclusion is terse. The title is only two words, the first line of the poem is a short, bleak statement. The second line begins with "iron bars". (Is it a door or gate? Perhaps the door had a little window with iron bars like those of a prison cell).

From the third line of stanza one and throughout stanza two, she describes the beauties of the garden in conventional terms (perhaps she could have tried harder to make it sound wonderful and exciting). The key word here is "mine" (repeated twice). In the last line of stanza two she states that it is now "lost".

The Bible tells us that we lose Paradise through sin. Adam and Eve were thrown out of Paradise for disobeying God and eating the forbidden fruit, and there are many references elsewhere, for example: 1 Corinthians 6:9-10: "Know ye not that the unrighteous shall not inherit the kingdom of God?" So perhaps Rossetti feels that she has sinned. Perhaps that sin was doubt. The Victorian period was a time of doubt because of the advances in science and technology, though this poem was published before the greatest blow to every religion was published: Charles Darwin's *On the Origin of Species* (1859).

It is a "shadowless spirit" who shuts her out. The description of this spirit is highly negative. The spirit is "shadowless", "blank", "unchanging", and the last adjective is qualified by the simile "like the grave". Whoever it is, it is certainly not Christ or the Holy Spirit or an angel. The nature of the spirit is open to interpretation, but it probably represents her own sin, or doubt.

The spirit does not even have the good manners to reply to her pleas when she begs for "one small twig from shrub or tree". Again, interpretation is difficult. In this allegory, what does the "small twig" represent? Could it be Grace, or absolution (the forgiveness of sins) that will remove the barrier between her and Paradise? The next two lines of this stanza show that she sees Paradise as her "home" (because she is a Christian) and that she will try again to get into it. In other words, she will try to stop committing the sin, or remove the doubts, that are the barrier between her and Paradise.

Once again, the bad-mannered spirit does not reply but builds a wall so that she can't even see in though she tries, emphasises by the word "straining". In the allegory, this perhaps means that she feels she cannot overcome her sin or doubt; that it is an impenetrable barrier between her and Paradise.

The next stanza describes her grief. She is "blinded with tears" because nothing else is worth looking at, especially as, by this time in her life (the poem was written in 1856), she has thrown away her chances of being happy in a human relationship.

The violets and the lark in the last stanza are example of earthly beauty, but they cannot compare with the birds and flowers of paradise described in stanza two; they are "not the best" and "not so dear". She develops the same idea more fully throughout the first two stanzas of *Paradise*:

> Once in a dream I saw the flowers
> That bud and bloom in Paradise;
> More fair they are than waking eyes
> Have seen in all this world of ours.
> And faint the perfume-bearing rose,
> And faint the lily on its stem,
> And faint the perfect violet
> Compared with them.

The tone of the poem is mournful and despairing. It must have been written during a period of deepest religious doubt.

Maude Clare

Out of the church she followed them
With a lofty step and mien:
His bride was like a village maid,
Maude Clare was like a queen.

"Son Thomas, " his lady mother said,
With smiles, almost with tears:
"May Nell and you but live as true
As we have done for years;

"Your father thirty years ago
Had just your tale to tell;
But he was not so pale as you,
Nor I so pale as Nell."

My lord was pale with inward strife,
And Nell was pale with pride;
My lord gazed long on pale Maude Clare
Or ever he kissed the bride.

"Lo, I have brought my gift, my lord,
Have brought my gift, " she said:
To bless the hearth, to bless the board,
To bless the marriage-bed.

"Here's my half of the golden chain
You wore about your neck,
That day we waded ankle-deep
For lilies in the beck:

"Here's my half of the faded leaves
We plucked from the budding bough,

With feet amongst the lily leaves, -
The lilies are budding now."

He strove to match her scorn with scorn,
He faltered in his place:
"Lady, " he said, – "Maude Clare, " he said, -
"Maude Clare, " – and hid his face.

She turned to Nell: "My Lady Nell,
I have a gift for you;
Though, were it fruit, the blooms were gone,
Or, were it flowers, the dew.

"Take my share of a fickle heart,
Mine of a paltry love:
Take it or leave it as you will,
I wash my hands thereof."

"And what you leave, " said Nell, "I'll take,
And what you spurn, I'll wear;
For he's my lord for better and worse,
And him I love Maude Clare.

"Yea, though you're taller by the head,
More wise and much more fair:
I'll love him till he loves me best,
Me best of all Maude Clare.

- mien – bearing or manner

QUESTIONS

1. This poem is written in the style of a traditional ballad.
   Re-read *Outlandish Knight* and compare the verse forms
   of the two texts.

2. Retell the story in your own words to make sure you have understood it.

3. What evidence is there that his mother has misgivings about the marriage?

4. What are the reasons that Thomas and Nell are pale?

5. Go through the whole poem, and make a list of differences between Nell and Maud. What do the similes in stanza one tell us about the two women?

6. What do we learn about the character of Thomas?

7. What gifts has Maude for Thomas? What can we guess from these gifts about what happened in the past? What message are they intended to give to Nell?

8. What happens when Thomas tries to stand up to her? What does this tell us about what Maude has to say?

9. How does Maude use the symbolism of fruit and flowers in stanza eight?

10. Nell's answer is surprising. What might we expect a woman to say in this situation? What does she actually say? Do you admire her for this, or think she is likely to end up as a subservient wife?

11. How is repetition used to good effect in the last verse?

12. If Maude really is "more wise and much more fair", why do you think Thomas chose Nell for a wife?

13. Of the two women, who do you think gets the better of the argument?

14. Compare and contrast this poem with *Love from the North*, which is also about a wedding.

COMMENTARY

Rossetti had a great fondness for traditional ballads, and often used ballad-form in her poetry (alternate tetrameter and trimeter with rhyme scheme a b c b). Often, she goes a step further and uses the narrative style and language of the traditional ballad, for example, the fast-paced narrative, the economical language, and archaic words like: "lo" and "yea".

From the first stanza we see that Maude is superior in many ways to Nell, though it is probably not an actual difference in status that is referred to as both are given the title, "lady" in the poem. We learn later on in the poem that Maude is taller, wiser and more beautiful. Why then is Thomas marrying Nell? Could the answer be in Maude's behaviour after the wedding when she forces a cruel confrontation. It could be argued that, if she had any sympathy at all for Thomas' new betrothed, she would have told her about his faults before the marriage, not after, when it was too late. Perhaps Thomas preferred the quality of subservience in a woman above all other qualities. The last two stanzas suggest this.

Maude's "gifts", described in stanzas four to eight, are a powerful way of getting her message across, as they are actual proof of a previous relationship in which promises were made on specific occasions which she describes in detail. Promises of marriage were taken very seriously in those days, and among the upper classes it sometimes happened that a man was sued for breach of promise.

Her gift to Nell is not a physical object, but is made almost physical by the way she uses the symbolism of fruit and flowers. If it were fruit, its "bloom" (freshness) would be gone. If it were flowers the dew would be gone ("dew" symbolising morning freshness). These symbols emphasise that Thomas' love is not "fresh", but second-hand. She goes on to spell out her meaning in literal terms: he is "fickle", and his love is "paltry" (too small in amount, having little meaning, or worth). She goes on to say "take it or leave it as you will", though, of course, she has left it too late (perhaps deliberately).

Nell's answer is not what we expect. She stands up for herself bravely. She sates that Maude had spurned him (with the suggestion that the break up of Maude and Thomas was not all his fault) and declares that she loves him. She shows insight in realises that, at that moment, Thomas probably still loves Maude the best, but states confidently that she will continue to love him until he loves her "the best". This phrase is repeated at the beginning of the next line to add emphasis, and to such effect, that we believe her. In effect, she wins the argument.

The poem is interesting to feminist critics because it portrays two strong women (and one weak man). Maude is not to be cast off easily as she is not lacking in the strength of character to fight back (in modern terms, she is "assertive"). On the other hand, Nell refuses to be intimidated by Maude, even though she is superior in many respects.

135

Up-Hill

Does the road wind up-hill all the way?
   Yes, to the very end.
Will the day's journey take the whole long day?
   From morn to night, my friend.

But is there for the night a resting-place?
   A roof for when the slow dark hours begin.
May not the darkness hide it from my face?
   You cannot miss that inn.

Shall I meet other wayfarers at night?
   Those who have gone before.
Then must I knock, or call when just in sight?
   They will not keep you standing at that door.

Shall I find comfort, travel-sore and weak?
   Of labour you shall find the sum.
Will there be beds for me and all who seek?
   Yea, beds for all who come.

QUESTIONS

1. The poem is written as a series of questions and answers. Who might be the speakers?

2. What is the "journey" in line three an allegory of?

3. What are the concerns of the questioner?

4. Are the answers reassuring?

5. Explain the allegory in simple, everyday words. For example, what does the title mean? What is the "resting-place"? Who are the other "wayfarers"? What is "that door"? What is referred to in the last stanza?

6. Describe the rhyme scheme of the poem.

7. Compare and contrast *Shut Out*, which is also an allegory.

8. Compare and contrast *Paradise: in a Dream* and/or *Shut Out*, in which heaven is described very differently.

9. Find out about *Pilgrim's Progress* by John Bunyan.

COMMENTARY

It is likely that this poem was inspired by the best-loved of Christian allegories, *Pilgrim's Progress* by John Bunyan (1678), and particularly the chapter entitled *The Hill Difficulty*. This is how that chapter begins:

I beheld, then, that they all went on till they came to the foot of the Hill Difficulty; at the bottom of which was a spring. There were also in the same place two other ways besides that which came straight from the gate; one turned to the left hand, and the other to the right, at the bottom of the hill; but the narrow way lay right up the hill, and the name of the going up the side of the hill is called Difficulty. Christian now went to the spring, and drank thereof, to refresh himself (Isa. 49:10), and then began to go up the hill...

Rossetti's poem is also an allegory in which the life of a Christian is compared to an up hill journey. It is presented in the form a dialogue between a Christian, who is asking the questions, and a respondent who is God or his representative, an angel ("Angel" means "messenger"). The lack of speech marks shows that the form is a *catechism*, which is a series of questions and answers used to teach doctrine.

We discover from the catechism that the journey will take "the whole day", in other words, the whole of a Christian's life. Day and night being life and death in the allegory.

The "resting place" is heaven, though it is described very differently in this poem by comparison with the descriptions in *Paradise: in a Dream* and *Shut Out* where garden imagery is used. Another feature of *Paradise: in a Dream* is that it is closely based on Biblical references. In the allegory in *Up-Hill*, heaven is compared to an inn where the Christian will meet "other wayfarers" (other Christians) and is reassured that non-one will be kept waiting at the door. In other words, the Christian soul will not face a period in some kind of limbo.

The questioner asks if there will be "comfort", and points out that he/she is travel-sore and weak?" The answer is difficult to interpret, but may mean that the Christian will be rewarded for his or her hard work in making the journey, in otherwise in avoiding sin and temptation. In the analogy, beds represent the desired repose after a difficult journey, and refer to the spiritual peace that the Christian soul will find in heaven.

The powerful simplicity of the analogy and the short questions and answers of the catechism form is reflected in the simple verse form. They rhyme scheme is a b a b. The rhythm is, appropriately, conversational, using a mix of iambs and anapaests.

138

Good Friday
(Am I a stone and not a sheep?)

Am I a stone and not a sheep
That I can stand, O Christ, beneath Thy Cross,
To number drop by drop Thy Blood's slow loss,
And yet not weep?

Not so those women loved
Who with exceeding grief lamented Thee;
Not so fallen Peter weeping bitterly;
Not so the thief was moved;

Not so the Sun and Moon
Which hid their faces in a starless sky,
A horror of great darkness at broad noon–
I, only I.

Yet give not o'er,
But seek Thy sheep, true Shepherd of the flock;
Greater than Moses, turn and look once more
And smite a rock.

NOTES

This poem, like many others in Rossetti's complete works, shows that she knew her Bible really well. A full understanding of the poem relies on a knowledge of the Biblical references:

The Women:

Matthew, Mark and John name some of the women who

attended the crucifixion. Mary, the mother of Jesus, is referred to by all three. Matthew and Luke refer to Mary the mother of James. John refers to two other Marys (Mary must have been a very popular name in those days!)

Peter:

Peter wept for Jesus when he denied him. This is described in Luke 22:61-62:

And the Lord turned, and looked upon Peter. And Peter remembered the word of the Lord, how he had said unto him, Before the cock crows, you shall deny me three times. And Peter went out, and wept bitterly.

The Thief:

The thief is described in all four gospels with some differences of detail. Here is Luke's account: (23:39-43):

Now one of the criminals hanging there reviled Jesus, saying, "Are you not the Messiah? Save yourself and us." The other, however, rebuking him, said in reply, "Have you no fear of God, for you are subject to the same condemnation? And indeed, we have been condemned justly, for the sentence we received corresponds to our crimes, but this man has done nothing criminal." Then he said, "Jesus, remember me when you come into your kingdom." He replied to him, "Amen I say to you today you will be with me in Paradise."

The Darkness:

The gospels of Matthew and Luke describe darkness at the time of the crucifixion. Here is Luke's account (Luke 23:44-46):

And it was about the sixth hour, and there was a darkness over all the earth until the ninth hour. And the sun was darkened, and the veil of the temple was rent in the midst. And when Jesus had cried with a loud voice, he said, Father, into thy hands I commend my spirit: and having said thus, he gave up the ghost.

If you have time, it is worth reading the story of Jesus' passion as a connected narrative. Luke's gospel is recommended (Chapters 22-23).

QUESTIONS

1. Explain the two key metaphors in the first line: "stone" and "sheep"? (Hint: think of how the words "sheep" and "shepherd" are used symbolically in the Bible).

2. How does Rossetti emphasise the slow, drawn-out suffering of crucifixion in line three of the first stanza?

3. How does Rossetti use key events from the Passion to elaborate the idea that she is a "stone" (viz., "hard hearted"). (Note: the word "Passion" is from the Latin: "passionem" and means "suffering". It is used to describe the events in Jesus' life from entry into Jerusalem to his crucifixion on Mount Calvary).

4. How does the last stanza pick up the ideas of the first? What is the effect of the subtle change from "stone" to "rock"?

5. Describe the verse form of the poem, and comment particularly on the emphasis given by the use of dimeter in stanzas one, three and four.

COMMENTARY

The poem is a good example of the devotional poetry which Rossetti wrote in later life. Like all her religious poems, it shows a very detailed knowledge of the Bible. The first line is based on two common Biblical symbols: "sheep" are the people, and (referred to in the last stanza) Christ is the "shepherd". (Jesus says in John 10:11: "I am the good shepherd: the good shepherd giveth his life for the sheep."). "Stone" was a common symbol for a hardened heart in the Bible (e.g., Ezekiel 36:26: I will give you a new heart, and I will put a new spirit within you. I will remove the heart of stone from your body and give you a heart of flesh.") Rossetti is asking herself why she can contemplate the crucifixion without weeping. Is it because she has a heart of stone instead of being a true follower of Christ?

In stanza two, she compares herself with the women who attended the crucifixion and with Peter. She ends by saying that even the thief was moved when he saw an innocent man crucified beside him.

In the third stanza she says, in a powerful personification, that even the sun and moon" hid their faces". She emphasises the darkness with the adjectives "starless" and "great". The dimeter that ends the stanza places emphasis on her own personal shortcoming (though I am sure that many other humans are similarly lacking – at least she is writing a poem about it!)

The final stanza refers to the Biblical idea of the "good shepherd", which she paraphrases here as "true shepherd". Such a shepherd will always try to save a lost member of his flock. She urges him to persevere in her difficult case ("give o'er" = "don't stop trying"). The allusion to Moses is interesting, because he was literally a shepherd before he went on to become a metaphorical shepherd in leading the Israelites out of Egypt.

The final line of the poem is a masterstroke. In a terse dimeter, further emphasise by rhyme, the poet refers back to the first line of the poem, and also alludes to another act of Moses:

And Moses lifted up his hand, and with his rod he smote the rock twice: and the water came out abundantly, and the congregation drank, and their beasts also. (Numbers 20:11)

There is also an echo (perhaps accidental) of John Donne's famous holy sonnet *Batter my Heart*. Using the concentrated power of all these poetical allusions and devices, Rossetti asks God to break her hard heartedness so that she can respond fully to the piteousness of the crucifixion.

Twice

I took my heart in my hand
(O my love, O my love),
I said: Let me fall or stand,
Let me live or die,
But this once hear me speak-
(O my love, O my love)-
Yet a woman's words are weak;
You should speak, not I.

You took my heart in your hand
With a friendly smile,
With a critical eye you scanned,
Then set it down,
And said: It is still unripe,
Better wait a while;
Wait while the skylarks pipe,
Till the corn grows brown

As you set it down it broke-
Broke, but I did not wince;
I smiled at the speech you spoke,
At your judgment that I heard:
But I have not often smiled
Since then, nor questioned since,
Nor cared for corn-flowers wild,
Nor sung with the singing bird.

I take my heart in my hand,
O my God, O my God,
My broken heart in my hand:
Thou hast seen, judge Thou
My hope was written on sand,

O my God, O my God:
Now let Thy judgment stand-
Yea, judge me now

This contemned of a man,
This marred one heedless day,
This heart take Thou to scan
Both within and without:
Refine with fire its gold,
Purge Thou its dross away-
Yea, hold it in Thy hold,
Whence none can pluck it out.

I take my heart in my hand-
I shall not die, but live-
Before Thy face I stand;
I, for Thou callest such:
All that I have I bring,
All that I am I give,
Smile Thou and I shall sing,
But shall not question much.

QUESTIONS

1. In what sense is the use of the word "heart" in the first line metaphorical?

2. Who is the first part of the poem addressed to? Who is the second part of the poem addressed to?

3. What do the repeated vocatives ("O") in line two of the first stanza and two of the fourth stanza emphasise?

4. Compare the tense of the first line of part one (stanza one) with the first line of part two (stanza 4). What does

this difference of tense tell us?

5. What words in stanza one show that the way her lover responds to the offer of her heart is crucial?

6. How does her lover respond to the offer of her heart? How does he look at her? What is his reason for rejecting the offer?

7. What is the effect of repeating the last word of line one in stanza one, at the beginning of the second line?

8. What does the metaphor "unripe" (stanza two, line five) mean?

9. What is the meaning of the metaphors in the lines: "Wait while the skylarks pipe,/ Till the corn grows brown."?

10. What was the result of this rejection (see stanza three). How did the narrator respond outwardly? How did she respond inwardly? What images are used to show this?

11. What is the shift of focus in part two of the poem (which begins in stanza four)?

12. What metaphor does she use to describe the fragility of her hope?

13. What words does she use to describe her heart in the first two lines of stanza five?

14. What does she ask God to do with her heart and what figurative language does she use to describe it?

15. Which lines in the poem reflect the generally accepted

view women's role in a relationship in the Victorian period? Which of her other poems offer a more assertive view?

16. Compare and contrast lines five and six of stanza six with the last stanza of *In the Bleak Midwinter*.

17. Describe the structure of the poem, including the verse form, the two-part structure and the repetition and parallelism.

COMMENTARY

Once again, Rossetti could be reflecting on one of her suitors in the 1850's (the poem was written in 1857). However, since it was Rossetti who did the rejecting, the poem may be written through the voice of a persona. Another interpretation is that it could refer to love that she felt when she was younger, and which was rejected. Even if the poem does not refer directly to Rossetti's own experiences, it is about a woman who, having been disappointed in human love, offers her heart (her love) to God, a transition that was important in Rossetti's life.

The poem is divided into two parts which echo and parallel each other. The first part describes how her love is rejected by a human lover and the second how her love is accepted by God.

The poem begins with a conventional metaphor. The depth of her love is demonstrated by the vocative "O my love" in line two. The importance of her love being accepted is seen in lines three and four which have two parallel opposites: "fall or stand" "live or die". The last two lines reflect the generally accepted view of women's role in a relationship in the Victorian period, which is quite different from the voice of the strong women (sometimes Rossetti's own) in many other poems.

Stanza two describes how her lover receives her offer. he is patronising: he has a "friendly eye" and "a critical smile". The words "scanned" is telling. It is as though he is looking at her, but only seeing her exterior, not her inner qualities. Not surprising, then, that he misjudges her, saying that she is immature ("unripe"). Two metaphors are used to say that it is better to wait until she is older. The skylark's song is associated with early summer, and harvest time (before the corn "turns brown" is in August. So the speaker is probably suggesting that she waits a few more months rather than years. Nevertheless, she feels rejected. Her heart is "broke", and this is emphasised by the immediate repetition of the word in the next line. She smiles outwardly, but her inner grief is described with nature imagery; she no longer has any joy in nature.

The beginning of part two of the poem parallels the beginning of part one, but with a significant change in tense. Rossetti uses the present tense to emphasise that offering her heart to God is what the narrator is doing now. The broken love affair is in the past. The vocative, which is perhaps stronger for not being in brackets, is repeated, but with the change to "God". In a conventional metaphor in line five she expresses a realisation that her hope for love was transitory, and goes on to say that God's judgement is permanent ("will stand"). She then asks God to judge her. This parallels the moment, described in stanza two, when her lover judged her.

In the next stanza she offers her heart (which has been "contemned: and "marred" by her lover) for God to "scan". The word echoes "scanned" in the same place in part one. It is imperfect, but God can purify it. This process is described in the imagery of metal refining. "Dross" means "mineral waste formed on the surface of molten metal". Gold is regarded as the purest metal (because it does not tarnish). The word "purge" however, has medical and Biblical associations, and is often linked with the word sin. Rossetti thus conflates in the these two lines the idea of purifying metal and purifying the body and soul. The last line of the stanza emphasises that her love is safe with God.

God's verdict is clearly favourable, for in the last stanza, Rossetti writes: "I shall not die, but live" (referring to eternal life). In lines five and six, she dedicates her love to God in words reminiscent of the last stanza of *In the Bleak Midwinter*. The penultimate line parallels the last line of the part one. Now she will sing with God, rather than the birds. The last line is perhaps the weakest line in the poem as it has lost the powerful parallelism with part one, and lacks a strong message. What she is saying is that she will not "question much" because she is secure and safe in the love of God.

Winter: My Secret

I tell my secret? No indeed, not I;
Perhaps some day, who knows?
But not today; it froze, and blows and snows,
And you're too curious: fie!
You want to hear it? well:
Only, my secret's mine, and I won't tell.

Or, after all, perhaps there's none:
Suppose there is no secret after all,
But only just my fun.
Today's a nipping day, a biting day;
In which one wants a shawl,
A veil, a cloak, and other wraps:
I cannot ope to every one who taps,
And let the draughts come whistling thro' my hall;
Come bounding and surrounding me,
Come buffeting, astounding me,
Nipping and clipping thro' my wraps and all.
I wear my mask for warmth: who ever shows
His nose to Russian snows
To be pecked at by every wind that blows?
You would not peck? I thank you for good will,
Believe, but leave that truth untested still.

Spring's an expansive time: yet I don't trust
March with its peck of dust,
Nor April with its rainbow-crowned brief showers,
Nor even May, whose flowers
One frost may wither thro' the sunless hours.
Perhaps some languid summer day,
When drowsy birds sing less and less,
And golden fruit is ripening to excess,

If there's not too much sun nor too much cloud,
And the warm wind is neither still nor loud,
Perhaps my secret I may say,
Or you may guess.

- ope – a poetic abbreviation for "open"
- languid – lacking energy or vitality

QUESTIONS

1. Who do you think is the speaker addressing?

2. Can you guess what the secret might be?

3. Look carefully at the vocabulary used to find evidence that this is "lovers' language".

4. What link does the speaker make between keeping her secret and keeping warm?

5. Can you find a hint that she might tell her secret in the future?

6. How does she use the seasons to tease her lover about when she might tell him her secret?

7. What is the secret?

8. This is a happy poem about a love which is still developing. Find another poem about happy love, and another about problems in love, and compare and contrast them with this one.

9. The verse form of the poem is irregular. Write out the rhyme scheme of one of the sections, and count the

number of stresses in each line. In particular, look carefully for internal rhyme. How does the irregular verse form suit the subject?

COMMENTARY

The speaker (who may or may not be Rossetti) seems to be addressing a man with whom she has some kind of love relationship (presumably in its early stages). We can deduce this from the teasing lovers' language that we find throughout the poem: "fie", "I won't tell", "just my fun", "you would not peck" (a peck is a quick kiss), "you may guess".

Throughout the poem, Rossetti uses the cold winter weather as an analogy for the onslaught of a lover. Most of the second strophe is a vivid description of the cold and the clothing she wears as a defence, using much internal rhyme. In the analogy, she says that she cannot open to everyone who knocks ("taps") because it would let the cold in. The "mask" she wears "for warmth" parallels the way she is hiding her inner self (and her secret) from her lover. "Russian snows" is a hyperbole to emphasise the severity of the winter, and this leads into the metaphor of being "pecked at" by the cold. This vividly describes the pinching sensation that temperatures below zero have on the face. In the next line, she picks up the word in an echo of her lover's answer: "You would not peck?" Here the word "peck" is used in its other sense of "a quick, light kiss". However, the last line asserts that she is not going to give him that chance.

In the last strophe, she continues her analogy by running through the seasons. Perhaps she will tell him her secret in Spring because it is "an expansive time", but she, still teasing, quickly adds that she doesn't trust March "with its peck of dust". Using the word "peck" to refer to the stinging sensation of dust blown in the face (and hinting of the kiss he is not allowed to have). May is also dangerous, because frost may wither the flowers. This seems to say that if she reveals her love too soon it might "wither". This teasing allegory builds up to a "languid summer day". "Languid" being illustrated by the birds who are too tired to sing and the fruit over-ripe. The weather is unthreatening "not too much sun nor too much cloud". Under these conditions, she might feel safe enough tell her secret. But the last line concludes with a challenge in which she is effectively saying. "You can wait that long, but you should be able to guess now." The secret is almost certainly that she loves him.

Soeur Louise De La Misericorde
(1674)

I have desired, and I have been desired;
  But now the days are over of desire,
  Now dust and dying embers mock my fire;
Where is the hire for which my life was hired?
  Oh vanity of vanities, desire!

Longing and love, pangs of a perished pleasure,
  Longing and love, a disenkindled fire,
  And memory a bottomless gulf of mire,
And love a fount of tears outrunning measure;
  Oh vanity of vanities, desire!

Now from my heart, love's deathbed, trickles, trickles,
  Drop by drop slowly, drop by drop of fire,
  The dross of life, of love, of spent desire;
Alas, my rose of life gone all to prickles,–
  Oh vanity of vanities, desire!

Oh vanity of vanities, desire;
  Stunting my hope which might have strained up higher,
  Turning my garden plot to barren mire;
Oh death-struck love, oh disenkindled fire,
  Oh vanity of vanities, desire!

- Soeur Louise De La Misericorde – Sister Louise
  of the Convent of Mercy

NOTE

The poem is about Louise de La Vallière (1644-1710)
who was a mistress of Louis XIV of France from 1661 to

1667. She later became the Duchess of La Vallière and Duchess of Vaujours in her own right. Louise was also very religious and became a Carmelite nun in June 1674. This is how Edward Bulwer Lytton, in the introduction to his play, Duchess de la Valliere, describes her life: "A sad progress from innocence to splendour – from the idolised to the deserted – from the deserted to the penitent and devout." What parallels can you find with Rossetti's life?

QUESTIONS

1. How is repetition used in the poem? (hint: begin by talking about the refrain?)

2. What does the repetition emphasise?

3. How is alliteration used in the poem?

4. Make a list of all the words that express negative feelings.

5. Explain the metaphor: "dying embers mock my fire".

6. What is the effect of the alliteration at the beginning of stanza two? How is this reinforced by the anaphora in the second line.

7. Explain the metaphor: "my heart, love's deathbed".

8. Compare the "rose" metaphor in stanza three with the same metaphor in stanza one of *A Daughter of Eve*.

9. "Garden plot" in stanza four is another metaphor she uses in *A Daughter of Eve*. Is it used in the same way?

10. "Death-struck love" in stanza four is one of the most powerful, almost shocking, expressions in the poem. What figure of speech is it? What is tis effect?

11. Describe the verse form of the poem. When writing out the rhyme scheme use "R" for the refrain.

12. Compare and contrast this poem with *A Daughter of Eve*.

COMMENTARY

In her poetry, Rossetti makes use of several different narrative perspectives. Sometimes she is writing in her own voice as in *No, Thank You, John*, sometimes we cannot be sure whether she is writing in her own voice or that of a created persona, for example, *Love from the North*. Sometimes she uses omniscient narrative, as in *Goblin Market* or *Jessie Cameron*. In this poem she is writing in the voice of a real person, but is clearly reflecting on her own life, as we can see from the parallels with *A Daughter of Eve*. The first two lines of this poem could also refer to Rossetti in her "year of love: (1850). She, too, feels that her youth (her "rose") has been wasted. She too feels that her "garden plot" (her health and beauty) has decayed, note the connotations of the word "barren".

She uses words from the Bible as a refrain: Ecclesiastes 1:2: "Vanity of vanities, saith the Preacher, vanity of vanities; all is vanity." Ecclesiastes is the Bible's book of wisdom. The word "vanity" has several meanings. Here it means "something that is empty or valueless". What she is saying is that desire is empty and valueless. The king desired her, she desired the king, but she was cast off in 1667. Though far less dramatic, Rossetti's own love affairs failed to prosper, and she had no more suitors after she turned down Charles Cayley in 1866.

These feelings are expressed in very powerful language with many words in the lexical field of suffering, sinking, dying, decaying. The imagery is vivid, the image of the dying or extinguished fire being used three times. Wasted youth and lost beauty are lamented in the image of the rose and the garden in a way that recalls a poem on a similar theme, *A Daughter of Eve*. Even death is brought into the imagery (on two occasions). The result is a tone of great bitterness and regret.

Essay and Examination Questions

1. "Far from being repressed, women in Rossetti's poems are powerful and independent." Discuss.

2. Compare and contrast any two of Rossetti's poems.

3. "Conflict is at the heart of the relationships between men and women in Rossetti's poetry." How far do you agree?

4. Explore the influence of traditional ballads on Rossetti's poetry.

5. Give an analysis of any two contrasting devotional poems.

6. Give an analysis of any two contrasting love poems.

7. "Goblin Market stands head and shoulders above Rossetti's other work." How far do you agree?

8. How does Rossetti use repetition in all its forms as a poetic technique in her poems?

9. How does Rossetti's poetry challenge conventional expectations of the role of women in Victorian society?

10. How far do you agree with the view that an overwhelming sadness hangs over Rossetti's poems?

11. How far is it possible to relate Rossetti's poems to her biography?

12. How is the female perspective presented in Rossetti's poems?

13. How is nature imagery used in Rossetti's poems?

14. "Rossetti is a strong woman who writes about strong women." Explore this idea.

15. Rossetti sometimes writes in her own voice and sometimes through the voice of a persona. Often we cannot be sure which is which, but they all have some relation to her life experiences. Discuss.

16. "Rossetti's devotional poetry presents life as a difficult struggle." Discuss.

17. "Rossetti's devotional poetry reflects the author's struggle with doubts about her own worthiness." Give examples and discuss.

18. Examine the use of different narrative perspectives in Rossetti's poems.

19. "Rossetti's imagery is often conventional, but she uses it to good effect." How far do you agree?

20. "Rossetti's life and her poetry have been negatively influenced by an almost fanatical devotion to religion." How far do you agree with this statement?

21. "Rossetti's narrative poems often reflect the author's life experiences, even though they may not be directly autobiographical." How far do you agree?

22. Show how Rossetti's poems explore all aspects of love, including sexuality.

23. Rossetti's poetry has been described as "pessimistic", but perhaps, in view of her life experiences, it is merely "realistic". What is your opinion?

24. "Rossetti's poetry is haunted by disappointment in love." How far do you agree?

25. "Rossetti is perhaps the most contradictory of the great Victorian poets." How far do you agree with this statement?

26. Show how Rossetti's disappointment in the love of man was transformed into a love of God.

27. "The mood of Rossetti's poems ranges from pessimistic to joyful." Give examples and discuss.

28. To what extent can Rossetti be described as a proto-feminist?

29. "Much of Rossetti's work is driven by uncertainty." Discuss.

30. What evidence can you find in Rossetti's poetry that she is a strong-minded, independent woman?

31. When Rossetti writes about the "battle of the sexes" the woman is usually the loser. How far is this a fair description of Rossetti's poems?

32. Rossetti's poetry is successful despite "its oppressive load of religious ideas." Discuss.

33. Write about one of the following themes in Rossetti's poetry: love, death, rejection, religion, the role of women.

34. Write about Rossetti's use dialogue and dramatic monologue.

35. Write about Rossetti's use of any two of the following techniques: rhyme, rhythm, repetition, imagery, symbolism, allegory, tone.

36. Write about Rossetti's use of any two of the following viewpoints: omniscient narrative, first person, third person, persona, autobiographical.

37. "Rossetti's poems seek nothing less than the mystery of Life and Death." How far do you agree with this statement?

38. Write about the way Rossetti uses sound in her poems with reference to some or all of the following: alliteration, assonance, consonance, onomatopoeia, sibilance, rhyme, internal rhyme, rhythm.

39. Rossetti often presents her ideas in dramatic form. Give examples and discuss the effect of this approach.

40. Write an introduction to the selection of Rossetti poems that you are studying.

ABOUT THE AUTHOR

In Conisbrough, in the West Riding,
I spent most of my childhood,
where there's an old castle, presiding
over the local neighbourhood.
The castle teased me with its mystery
and got me interested in history.
Then at Leeds university
I took a literature degree,
Choosing an option of Jane Austen
and Regency Society,
And also one on poetry:
worlds which I loved to get lost in
so much, I cannot live without them –
and so I try to write about them.

Chris Webster
Singapore
2016

Printed in Poland
by Amazon Fulfillment
Poland Sp. z o.o., Wrocław